CRUSHING THE
COMMON APP
ESSAY

CRUSHING THE COMMON APP
ESSAY

A Foolproof Guide

to Getting into

Your Top College

JULIE FERBER FRANK

For my mom, and in memory of my dad,
who made me feel I could accomplish anything . . .
. . . and for my beloved Steven, Sophie, Sam, and Mia,
who make me feel I want to accomplish everything.

© 2018 Sterling Publishing Co., Inc.
Cover © 2018 Sterling Publishing, Co., Inc.

ISBN 978-1-4114-7910-4

Distributed in Canada by Sterling Publishing Co., Inc.
c/o Canadian Manda Group, 664 Annette Street
Toronto, Ontario, M6S 2C8, Canada
Distributed in the United Kingdom by GMC Distribution Services
Castle Place, 166 High Street, Lewes, East Sussex, BN7 1XU, England
Distributed in Australia by NewSouth Books
45 Beach Street, Coogee, NSW 2034, Australia

For information about custom editions, special sales, and premium
and corporate purchases, please contact Sterling Special Sales at
800-805-5489 or specialsales@sterlingpublishing.com.

Manufactured in Canada

Lot #:
2 4 6 8 10 9 7 5 3 1
03/18

sterlingpublishing.com
sparknotes.com

Please submit all comments and questions or report errors to
sparknotes.com/errors

Contents

PROLOGUE   9

INTRODUCTION   13

WORDS THAT MATTER   16

CHAPTER 1: **THE BIG PICTURE**   19
What Are Colleges Looking For?   19
What Your Essay Should Do for You   21

CHAPTER 2: **THE FOUR BUILDING BLOCKS OF A COMMON APP ESSAY**   22
Building Block #1: Five Words   22
Building Block #2: Story   23
Building Block #3: Message   25
Building Block #4: Archetype   30

CHAPTER 3: **THREE SAMPLE ESSAYS AND ANALYSIS**   36
Abby's Common App Essay   36
Jackson's Common App Essay   41
Ella's Common App Essay   46

CHAPTER 4: **HOW TO FIND YOUR TOPIC**   52
Story Prompts   52
Questions to Help You Find Your Story   53
Big Impacts   57
A Unique Point of View   63
Accentuate the Positive   69
Intellectual Vitality   74
Learning Differences   79
Creativity   86
Think Outside the Box   90

CHAPTER 5: **OUTLINING YOUR ESSAY**   95
Structure, Structure, Structure!   95
Three Sample Structures   97
Pick a Tense   101

CHAPTER 6: **IT'S ALL IN THE DETAILS**   107
Voice   107
The All-Important First Sentence   108
Quotes   112
Emotion   113

Courage 120
Framing Device 125
Making the Most of This Wonderful Opportunity 130

CHAPTER 7: **A STEP-BY-STEP GUIDE TO WRITING YOUR COMMON APP ESSAY** 134

CHAPTER 8: **THOSE DARNED SUPPLEMENTALS** 144

EPILOGUE 147

APPENDIX A: **TWO SAMPLE ESSAYS OF EACH ARCHETYPE** 149
The Hero 151
The Seeker 158
The Adventurer 165
The Rebel 172
The Dreamer 179
The Caregiver 186
The Artist 192
The Leader 199
APPENDIX B: **ANOTHER UNIQUE POINT OF VIEW** 206

APPENDIX C: **SAME TOPIC, DIFFERENT RESULT** 211

APPENDIX D: **ART SCHOOL** 215

APPENDIX E: **THINK OUTSIDE ANOTHER BOX** 218

APPENDIX F: **WHEN YOUR STORY IS BIGGER THAN A SINGLE MOMENT** 222

APPENDIX G: **THE EVOLUTION OF AN ESSAY** 227

APPENDIX H: **WHERE'D THEY LAND?** 243

BIG THANKS 247

INDEX 249

THREE SIMPLE TRUTHS

1. Plenty of fine books have been written on the topic of writing the college application essay.

2. Many are more than 500 pages long.

3. No self-respecting teenager will read a 500-page book to write a 650-word essay.

PROLOGUE

BY THE TIME I was in my mid-twenties, I'd lived in Berkeley, Paris, New York City, and Los Angeles. I'd interned at *ABC News*, danced to house music in Moscow, waited tables off the Champs-Élysées, proofread million-dollar contracts in a Manhattan skyscraper, performed Molière in French in sixteen states, photographed cheetahs in Africa, cycled around Paramount Studios while running errands for a sitcom staff, and ghostwritten TV pilot pitches for a retired soap opera producer. But when I learned about a brand new graduate screenwriting program at USC Film School that I desperately wanted to get into and discovered I had only forty-eight hours to write my personal statement, I panicked.

Nothing in my preceding twenty-six years had prepared me for this task: not prep school, not college, and definitely not the oddball assortment of jobs I'd thrown myself into since graduation. Up to that moment, I'd done plenty of academic writing, more research papers and literary analysis than I cared to remember, and even my fair share of stories and scripts. But how was I supposed to know how to write this kind of personal assessment, revealing both my big picture and my specific quirks and strengths in a limited number of words?

Facing this insane deadline, I buckled down, caffeinated up, and somehow managed to write an essay that got me in.

Thrilled, I heaved a huge sigh of relief, thinking I'd never again have to deal with this kind of application essay.

Flash forward many years to a night in late December when my brother called in a panic. His beloved niece on his wife's side of the family was about to click Submit on her Common App, and she asked him to read her essay. When he did, he wasn't impressed. So he called me—the writer in the family—to ask if I'd take a look. Ten minutes later, I'd finished the draft. Her essay was a clever riff on how her life's greatest struggle had been that she'd never experienced any struggle . . . which, regrettably, told me absolutely nothing about what she had experienced. I called my brother's niece to say, "I've never met you, and I don't know a thing about you, but I'm certain you have a better story to tell and a more important message to deliver than what's on this page." She could have hung up on me, but instead she listened to my concerns and agreed that she could do better. We spent the next four days on the phone as I coached her through brainstorming, writing, and rewriting a powerful and deeply personal new essay.

As soon as my friends heard I'd helped one high school senior, they started asking me to help more. Before I knew it, a project was born. Working over several years with every imaginable kind of student, I've learned countless lessons about how to facilitate this process. I've also discovered one universal truth: no one wants to make this onerous task take longer than it has to. So I developed a fast-paced, foolproof system for writing compelling personal statements. And when the number of students asking for my guidance became more than I could manage, I distilled my method into this quick and (I hope!) entertaining guide. It's long enough to help you capture what's distinct about you and share it with the gatekeepers of your desired future and short enough to ensure you get it done in days. So sit back and enjoy the read. Because who doesn't love a good story?

INTRODUCTION

YOU MIGHT THINK having a mom who coaches students on their college application essays would leave my daughter Sophie sitting pretty her senior year. But do you know how many of Sophie's essays I read before she clicked *Submit*?

Zero. That's how many she let me read. And don't think I didn't try.

"Hey, Soph, how about I take a little peek? I could assess your structure. Check your language. Proofread your grammar."

"No thanks, Mom."

"Really, you're not going to let me read them at all?"

"Oh, you can read them. After I get accepted and you and Dad send in the deposit."

Her independence, which I usually applauded, was killing me. But in that moment, she needed me to be her mom, not her coach.

What Sophie did allow me to do was sit her down and have "the talk." My version of "the talk" skips right past the birds and the bees and cuts to the *really* juicy stuff: the tools, insights, and shortcuts that'll speed you to a killer essay. It's what I gave to Sophie. And it's what I'm about to give to you.

Before we dive in, I'd like to make three points. First, no matter who you are, where you come from, or where you're going, you have a great Common App essay in you. If you're a living, breathing, thinking human being, you have a meaningful story to share about your unique life experience. So have confidence in yourself and meet this process with both pride and focused effort.

Second, you might think you already know what you want to write about. If so, do me a favor: write down your idea . . . and then set it aside. Read this book with an open mind. And when you get to the end, if you're still convinced that your original idea is the best story to illustrate your most crucial message, then use it! On the other hand, if while reading the book you discover an even better story that delivers a more unique and vital message, embrace that. In either case, you'll be guaranteed to make smart, well-informed choices along your way to an impactful essay.

Third, as my dad used to say, all things worth doing are worth doing well. As you move through this book, examining the large and small experiences and themes of your life, it's important that you take time to be thoughtful. Allow yourself moments to contemplate. Let your ideas stew. Writing your Common App essay demands big things of you, so don't race through it just to be done. While you're working, take breaks. Walk your dog. Draw a picture. Meditate, if that's your thing. If you ask yourself significant questions and then give yourself some breathing room, your subconscious mind might just offer up the answers. Remember, brainstorming and rigorously challenging your ideas are the hardest parts of the job; if you do them well, the last part—writing and rewriting—will be a breeze.

So exactly how will we get from here (swirling chaos and anxiety) to there (a polished essay that shares something essential about who you are)? We'll do it chapter by chapter. In the first six chapters of this book, I'll lay out everything you need to know to write a successful personal statement: what you want your essay to accomplish, the four building blocks of a great essay, sample essays and analysis so you see how and why they work, different ways to find your story, how to structure your essay, and the details that will make it great. In the seventh chapter, I will lead you through a brief, practical, step-by-step guide to actually writing your essay. If you complete every step, your essay will be done.

So take a deep breath, and read on.

WORDS THAT MATTER

THERE ARE a lot of words in this book. The following are the ones that matter most. Do yourself a favor, and read them out loud.

message	authenticity
character	emotion
passion	leadership qualities
purpose	suspense
embracing of diversity	conflict
bridge-building	vivid descriptions
curiosity	sincerity
intellectual vitality	enthusiasm
adaptability	intentionality
resilience	struggle
willingness to change	growth
willingness to take chances	confidence
achievement	new understanding
generosity	initiative
ambition	impact
work ethic	one colorful, lively story

beginning, middle, ending	accomplishments
motivation	goals
drive	appreciation of nature
making choices	appreciation of culture
taking actions	pattern of service
innovation	maturity
creativity	sensitivity
originality	voice
honesty	open-mindedness
humor	unique quality

As you move through this book, you'll see these words, phrases, and ideas everywhere and learn they are the vital qualities you want to illustrate in your Common App essay. By the time you reach the end of this book, you'll understand why.

CHAPTER 1

THE BIG PICTURE

You probably know that the Common App essay prompts can change from year to year, but the themes don't. They always offer an opportunity to write about a time you took a chance or experienced failure and what you learned from it, a time you challenged the status quo and took action, something that caused you to mature and grow, or any quality or experience that's central to who you are. Given that these prompts are so broad and open-ended, the good news is you can feel free to write about almost anything. But first, let's be strategic and ask . . .

What Are Colleges Looking For?

Colleges are in the business of creating communities. That's a little like being a mad scientist who's forging a new and ideal world. As they choose who'll populate and define their world, what are they looking for? Students who've proven themselves to be bright, ambitious, hardworking, open-minded, and generous. More specifically, they seek people who have demonstrated the following:

* **Character**: enthusiastic students who do the right thing, exhibit good judgment, and follow through on commitments

* **Passion:** students who care about something—anything—and pursue it with gusto

* **Purpose**: students who engage, show initiative, take action, and have an impact

* **Diversity** (of race/culture/geography/thought/perspective/vision/experience): students who not only tolerate difference but also embrace it, exhibit social courage and curiosity, seek out all kinds of people, and build bridges

* **Intellectual vitality**: students who love to learn, possess a powerful hunger for knowledge and understanding, and are deeply excited to use their minds in new ways to make meaningful connections

* **Dedication and generosity**: students who reveal a deep and long-term pattern of getting involved and serving others

* **Adaptability and resilience**: students who encounter a challenge, obstacle, big life change, or failure and find ways to learn from it, adapt, and grow

What Your Essay Should Do for You

Given that so much of the application is filled with scores, stats, and cold hard facts, the essay is your one and only chance to step out of the data pool and introduce yourself as a full-fledged human being. It lets you share who you are, what you think about, and all you feel. It also allows you to create a narrative that unifies your whole application.

When done right, your essay couldn't be written by any other person on this planet because it's an honest, thoughtful, and clear expression—in your own voice—of who you are.

CHAPTER 2

THE FOUR BUILDING BLOCKS OF A COMMON APP ESSAY

To craft a Common App essay, you'll need four main building blocks:

* Five words that best describe you on your best day
* A story
* A message
* An archetype

Let's explore these pieces one at a time.

Building Block #1: Five Words

Before you can begin to *share* yourself, you must *know* yourself. So grab a paper and pen and jot down a list of **five words that best describe you on your best day**. Don't overthink it. There's no right or wrong. Just write. Are you funny, generous, creative, analytical, playful, kind, curious, loyal, optimistic, silly, courageous, ambitious, disciplined, gleeful, tenacious, free-spirited, shy, uninhibited, inclusive, outrageous, fierce, caring, imaginative, outgoing, hardworking, calm, powerful, inspiring, independent, or fearless? If not, figure out what you are and write it down.

While we're at it, I'd like you also to make a list of the

five words that best describe you on your worst day. Are you sad, angry, impatient, outraged, frustrated, hopeless, stubborn, exhausted, lonely, downtrodden, nervous, bummed, afraid, isolated, or pissed off? These descriptors and feelings might remind you of specific moments when you faced real challenges and/or obstacles and ultimately decided to change course, take new actions, and grow.

Great, now set aside the two lists. We'll come back to them later.

Building Block #2: Story

If you're bummed you have to chain yourself to a desk to write a long, dry, boring essay, I'm here to say, "No, you don't." In fact, I say, "No, you may not." Instead, I'm going to challenge you to tell a story—one colorful, lively story.

Why a story? Because for the person on the admissions committee staring down a stack of 500 essays, reading a story is the most entertaining, pleasing, and compelling way to take in information.

What kind of story should you tell? It's got to be **authentic**. Colleges *want* to get to know you. They literally have only a few minutes to give you their attention, so make the most of those minutes by revealing your real and best self.

Your story should be **moving**. *Feeling* makes a story vibrant and memorable, and it conveys how much the writer cares about something and is engaged in it.

Your story must reveal your unique **character**, **passion**, and **purpose**. As we know, that's what colleges are looking for. So . . . ask yourself: Are you the person who sticks up for the underdog? Convinces your lunchtime crew to recycle? Creates a website or blog to explore what the students in your high school really think? Shaves your head in solidarity with a classmate being treated for cancer? Inspires the math team to crunch numbers or musical cast to earn a standing ovation or varsity team to take home the trophy? Joins a protest against intolerance or for equality? Rocks a panther costume as the school mascot because you don't care if the crowd is laughing at you, so long as they're laughing? Lets down a friend, regrets it, and then finds a way to make it right? Remember, colleges believe that your behavior in the past will predict your behavior in the future. So share what you've already done to intrigue them with what will come.

Your story might illustrate your **intellectual vitality** in and out of the classroom. Do you attend a monthly book club or annual Latin convention? Do you watch YouTube videos on neuroscience, listen to NPR podcasts on economics, repost NASA tweets about the Mars Rover, or visit reptile shows? Do you write letters to ask questions of favorite authors or activists or artists? When you're curious about something, what actions do you take?

Your story might show you as a person who **leads**. This doesn't have to be in an obvious way—you don't have to be student body president. It can be in a quiet, subtle way. Maybe you're the first one on campus to invite a new student to join your group for lunch. Or perhaps you're the lacrosse player who, by volunteering to collect balls and take down the goals after an exhausting practice, unintentionally inspires your teammates to pitch in too. In any case, you want your story to show how you not only fulfilled your own potential but inspired others to fulfill theirs as well.

Your story must include some **conflict**. Every tale worth telling includes difficulty that challenges us and changes who we are. And every good writer knows that no narrative good comes from smooth sailing.

Your story should illustrate your **resilience** and ability to **change**. Don't be afraid to share that as you pursue goals and encounter obstacles, you sometimes make mistakes, falter, and even fail. But then you learn, grow, and evolve. Colleges want your experiences in their classrooms and on their campuses to change you. Show them that you have the willingness and capacity to change.

Most important of all, your story should reveal what **unique quality** you will bring to the college community. Colleges like to know what they'll get if they accept you. So paint a vivid picture of how you'll dig in if you get onto their campus: curiously learning, actively participating, and meaningfully contributing in ways that only you can.

And just so you know, no essay will show every one of these things. But every essay should include **struggle**, **growth**, **change**, and **new understanding**.

Building Block #3: Message

When I sit down to work with students, they often know their essay should contain a story. What they usually *don't* know is that it must also include a **message**. Your message is what you want your reader to walk away knowing about you in your truest place. To find it, you want to reflect on yourself and your experiences until you can articulate something important about who you are—the theme, message, drive, or point of view that gives your life great personal meaning.

I think the easiest way to learn this lesson is by example. Here we go.

While drafting a personal statement for her state college, a student named Rosie was asked to write about an interesting experience. She wrote about traveling in Sicily with her uncle and cousin. One day they went to visit a quarry to see where stone was turned into huge, round columns. The next day they went to see the ruins of a half-built ancient temple that the columns had been intended for. It was a nice story—very well written, with beautiful descriptions, but one concern gnawed at me. So when she asked what I thought, I voiced it.

"It's a nice story," I said, "but why are you telling it to me?"

"Because the application said I have to write about an interesting experience."

"Why this one?"

"Because it was a really cool place?" she replied.

That's when I explained that when a school asks you to describe an interesting experience, they care less about the specific experience and more about why *you* found it interesting.

I asked Rosie why she found this experience interesting.

She said, "Well, the day we went to the quarry, we were literally the only three people there. The next day, when we went to the temple, there was a huge crowd of people. It made me a little sad that all those people at the temple missed the experience of going to the quarry and seeing where the columns came from."

"Why did it make you sad?"

"I guess because I like to know where things come from," she answered. "I like to know the source. It's like when I cook. I like to go to the farmers market to meet the growers and learn about their farms and what's in season. It's like when I took a bookbinding class. I love reading and books so much, I wanted to learn how books are literally put together."

And I smiled. Because I knew, with a little digging, Rosie had discovered her **message**, a point of view that's unique to her, gives meaning to her experiences, and makes her life richer:

I am an inquirer who dives beneath the surface in pursuit of a deeper understanding.

Then Rosie handed me a supplemental essay she'd written. The prompt asked her to describe her family. She'd written a funny story about the road trip her family takes each summer. The depiction of the five of them and the dogs crammed in the car for twenty hours was lively. But when I got to the end, I asked her the same question I'd asked earlier: "Why are you telling me this?"

Rosie started to say, "Because they told me to describe

my fam—" but she stopped herself, because she wasn't a fool. She thought about what she'd learned from the previous essay. And she said, "Oh, I did it again. I told you a *story* but I didn't articulate my *message*."

I asked her what her message about her family might be.

She thought and replied, "Maybe my message is that even though we're all five so different, we're still happy to spend time together."

So I asked her for a single story that might illustrate that truth about her family, and she described one specific stop on a road trip they'd taken. "In Ashland, Oregon, we all wanted to do different things: my sister wanted to swim in an ice cold lake, my brother wanted to go zip-lining, I wanted to see a Shakespeare play. But instead of splitting up, we all agreed to each pick one activity and be a good sport while we were doing everyone else's activity. And we all ended up having fun together and trying something new."

Rosie had found her **message** about her family:

We're five very different people who treasure the richness that comes from sticking together.

To help you grasp this concept, I've made a list of the messages of a dozen former students. As you read them, picture these kids standing on a mountaintop shouting out their messages: the things they've discovered that matter most to them.

Through struggling with dyslexia, I've become a

28

person who takes nothing for granted and works every day to support my own growth.

I am an outrageous pursuer of business opportunities.

I'm a child of adoption who's discovered that we don't choose the circumstances into which we are born, but we do choose what we make of them.

I live at the intersection of imagination and computer programming.

I am an optimist, greeting unexpected curveballs with openness, curiosity, and wonder.

I am a team captain who refuses to lose faith in the power of hard work and the dream of leading my team to success.

I am a shy individual who's learned that the only way to truly become part of a community is to take a chance and share myself with others.

I am a survivor. Losing four years of life to misdiagnoses and ineffective treatments would make some people angry; I choose to move forward with joy.

I am the younger sister of triplet brothers who fights for equality for all.

I am an inquirer who has happily discovered that the more I learn, the less I know.

I am a girl who had to search for new reasons to live after my best friend died.

I'm the person who is going to get humanity off this rock and into space where we belong, because I can get things done.

Remember, as you write your essay, your message is your thesis that your story proves true.

Building Block #4: Archetype

When I help students brainstorm possible messages, I like to use a tool called archetypes. Archetypes are universally recognized characters found in myths and stories that transcend all time, location, and culture (stick with me here, you'll be glad you did):

The Hero	**The Dreamer**
The Seeker	**The Caregiver**
The Adventurer	**The Artist**
The Rebel	**The Leader.**[1]

---

1 The concept of psychological archetypes was explored in the early twentieth century by the Swiss psychiatrist Carl Jung. He proposed that each archetype represents a unique aspect of the collective unconscious. Jung wrote about archetypes as patterns of behavior that come from instinct. So an archetype is a distinct, recognizable, instinctive way to be.

When we see these personality types in a story, we relate to them. Right away we know who they are and what they want. We *get* them . . . just like we want the college admissions officers to *get* us. And we *root* for them . . . just like we want the college admissions officers to *root* for us. Archetypes are a kind of human shorthand: powerful, effective, and clear.

Though there are many archetypes, we're going to focus on these eight.

To start, let's look at a thumbnail sketch of each of these characters. As we do, ask yourself:

* Does this sound like me?

* Is what makes this archetype tick what makes me tick too?

* Is what gets them up in the morning and keeps them up late at night what gets me up and keeps me up too?

If so, you might have discovered the archetype that will help you launch your essay.[2]

---

2 Here I'd like to send a huge thank-you to Margaret Mark and Carol S. Pearson for their insightful, incisive book *The Hero and the Outlaw: Building Extraordinary Brands through the Power of Archetypes* (New York: McGraw-Hill, 2001). In it, they build on Jung's work to define age-old archetypes and explore how they can help in modern-day marketing and branding. For our purposes, we will study how these age-old archetypes can help in modern-day college application essay writing.

The Hero A resilient, ambitious crusader who takes courageous, difficult action to improve the world and prove his/her worth	**The Seeker** An inquirer and thinker who seeks truth and understanding through information and knowledge; pursues wisdom, confidence, and mastery; and promotes continuous learning	**The Adventurer** A slightly restless and deeply curious individualist who explores the world to find out who he/she is and seeks new experiences, joyful discovery, freedom, and authenticity with an open mind
The Rebel An outsider who revolts against what isn't working for him/herself or society and goes outside conventional behavior and morality to disrupt, change, and liberate	**THE EIGHT ARCHETYPES**	**The Dreamer** An innocent who seeks happiness and fulfillment through faith, hope, and optimism; desires simplicity and goodness; finds renewal in nature; and is calm, a bit naïve, and positive
The Caregiver A nurturer who has a passion to help, comfort, and protect others from harm; is filled with compassion and generosity; and has concern for others and the larger world	**The Artist** An innovator who uses imagination and creativity to bring beauty, culture, and form to the world; a nonconformist who loves to express him/herself and bring his/her vision to life	**The Leader** A role model who takes control to lead a group to success and prosperity; acts with an innate authority that makes others want to follow; takes responsibility for making life stable; and reinforces order

Archetypes are personality types based on how a person thinks and takes action. One isn't better or more advantageous than another—either in life or in Common App essay writing. They're all interesting and compelling and passionate and moving for completely different reasons. They're also useful in helping you find your message.

In a way, selling yourself to colleges is much like selling a product in a marketplace. In this case, you are the product. The archetype you choose is your brand. It defines you and brings clarity to what you're offering. It allows you to differentiate yourself from others. And in the college essay writing world, the archetype you choose will act as a compass guiding you to the **message** you'll deliver to the college admissions officers. [3]

---

[3] When you've reached the end of this book, if you're interested in seeing sample essays for each archetype, take a look at appendix A.

My husband, Steven, likes to joke that the best possible day in the world for me would be if he handed me a plane ticket in a sealed envelope and told me to go the airport, hand over the envelope, and get on a plane to an unknown destination. And he's right. Because I am an Adventurer.

He also jokes that the worst possible day in the world for my oldest friend would be if he handed her a plane ticket in a sealed envelope and told her to go to the airport, hand over the envelope, and get on a plane to an unknown destination. And he's right. Because while my friend is monumentally kind and thoughtful and curious about the world, she is even more monumentally nervous about trying anything new. She is not an Adventurer.

You are who you are. The trick is figuring out who you are and revealing it in a story.

So if I'm an Adventurer and I have to write a college application essay, I know my message will somehow relate to seeking new experiences, how *that* is what makes me feel most alive. I'll start to brainstorm every meaningful experience I've had in high school that reveals me to be an Adventurer, being open to and seeking novelty and possibility and finding meaning in discovery. (Remember, though it's okay to write briefly about how you were inspired by something that happened when you were younger, your main story should illustrate how you've taken action since you've been in high school.) I'll explore all the life experiences I've had—especially *choices I've made* and *actions I've taken*—that reveal me to be an Adventurer. I'll make a list of those experiences, and if I get stuck, I'll think about the moments in my life when I felt the greatest joy or worst fear or most profound connection to others or to nature. Because as a general rule of thumb, if you felt big feelings in the moment, your story can be written to convey great personal meaning and heart.

*****

Okay, enough with the abstract ideas. Let's see how they work in the concrete world by reading and analyzing three sample essays. At this point, don't worry about *how* these students found their stories; we will discuss that process in depth later. Instead, focus on what you can learn from them about solid storytelling and clearly illustrated messages.

CHAPTER 3

THREE SAMPLE ESSAYS AND ANALYSIS

The first sample essay we're going to look at was written by Abby, an accomplished, upbeat, and social student. After studying all the archetypes, she decided she was an Adventurer—restless, curious, and driven to seek novelty and authenticity.

Abby grew up in a small city in the Pacific Northwest. She didn't have the benefit of exotic trips around the world, but she did manage to be an Adventurer in her daily life. And that's what she decided to write about in her essay.[4]

Abby's Common App Essay

I have exactly 891 friends on Facebook. I've been class president, yearbook editor, and dance team captain. I'm the girl who can be friends with anyone and is friends with everyone. I move from group to group, know the unspoken rules, and play the social games. But I'm also the girl who wonders, "What if?"

---

4 Please note that there are an infinite number of ways to live as an Adventurer—depending on your personality, talents, limits, and setting—just as there are an infinite number of ways to live as each other archetype. That's the fun of archetypes: exploring your one-of-a-kind expression of your archetype's universal instincts.

It's Halloween during my junior year. Feeling fed up with all the social dividers, I decide to take a chance. I invite over my favorite friends from three different groups. In school, they travel in separate circles and don't give each other the time of day. One is a fun-loving blonde, another is a jokester, and the last is a guy who solves math equations for fun.

As soon we are all in a room together, I realize this is a very bad idea. No one speaks. Awkwardness encases us. The small talk feels forced. Finally, someone has the brilliant idea to go do something none of us has ever done before. We decide to explore a local corn maze.

When we arrive at the entrance, we step inside, unsure and excited. It's extremely dark and hard to see anything. I feel tiny, surrounded by the towering corn. We keep coming to splits in the road, making choices, not knowing whether we are going in the right or wrong direction. We find ourselves moving as a unit, deciding together which way to go. Finally, we stop. We look at each other and, without words, acknowledge that we are totally and completely lost. Just then, rain starts pouring down on us. Not knowing what to do, we take each other's hands and move forward.

After a minute, the path opens to a clearing, and then I see it. A haystack. It rises high above us. Could this be the thing to save us? We exchange glances. And in silence, we all start to climb, pushing and pulling each other up. When we reach the top, we look down at the maze and clearly see our way home. Standing together at the peak, we are exhausted, drenched, united, and triumphant.

I break out laughing with delight. My friends echo my laughter. We feel alive and connected, as if time has stopped. We feel free.

When I invited over these very different friends, I wasn't sure what would happen. I was afraid that it wouldn't work out. But once we made our way to the top of the haystack, I felt like I wasn't alone.

It isn't always easy to take risks. It can be scary and hard to open up to the unknown. But on that Halloween night, by saying "What if?" I discovered that so much is possible. In my lifetime, I want to connect with all kinds of different people. And I learned the best way to do that is to take a chance and let myself ask the most simple and beautiful question of all: "What if?"[5]

---

5 If you're curious about the building blocks of Abby's essay, here they are:
Five Best-Day Words: outgoing, upbeat, diligent, curious, kind
Story: bringing unlikely friends together in a corn maze on Halloween night
Message: I want to reach out to and connect with all kinds of people.
Archetypes: Leader, Seeker, Adventurer

What can we learn from Abby?

The first thing you probably notice is that nowhere in her essay does Abby announce, "I am an Adventurer!" She doesn't have to. By subtly and strategically using the Adventurer archetype to help guide her choice of story and message, Abby lets the reader discover that she's an Adventurer without ever having to be told.

What else do you notice about the essay? Obviously, it's written in the **authentic voice** of a seventeen-year-old. No big words from the thesaurus. No false points of view. Just clear, thoughtful, **conversational communication** from a real, live person.

Abby's story has a distinct **beginning, middle, and ending**. She and her friends decide to go to the corn maze; they get lost in the corn maze; they discover their way out of the corn maze.

Abby's story has **suspense and conflict**. When the kids realize they're lost, they know they're in trouble. Even if the trouble isn't life-threatening, it infuses the story with tension and raises the stakes.

Abby uses plenty of **imagery** to bring the story to life. She references the towering corn, deep darkness, and pouring rain. All those specific descriptions pull the reader into the story.

Abby is **confident**. She takes a chance, writes about an experience that's deeply personal, and reveals her most genuine self.

Abby is **honest**. She doesn't pretend to have all the answers, but she does reveal herself to be a thinking, feeling, questioning person. She willingly admits to **struggles** big and small, like her frustration with social divides and her inability to find her way out of the corn maze. She also highlights her **strengths**, like her many friends and curiosity about people. This honest, thoughtful inclusion of both struggle and strength shows that she is authentic and real.

Abby is **unprejudiced and unbiased**. She likes that her friends are all so different. That's a good thing to share because, as we know, colleges want students who not only tolerate but also embrace diversity. Abby also shows she is a **bridge builder**. Another plus.

Abby uses **humor** to draw in the reader. When she describes one friend as a *guy who solves math equations for fun* and confesses *As soon we are all in a room together, I realize this is a very bad idea*, she wins over her reader.

Abby chooses a story that shows **how she relates to and behaves in the world.** It illustrates how she deals with difficulty (when her group is at its lowest point, she takes her friends' hands and moves forward with united perseverance). It reveals what questions she's wrestling with (*can I break through social expectations?*) and what answers she's discovering (*yes!*). And it clearly articulates how she finds meaning in life (*reaching out to diverse people sets me free*).

Abby understands that admissions officers **care less about what you've done in your lifetime and more about how you think about what you've done**. No one gets into a college because they found their way through a corn maze.

But Abby did because of the thoughtful way she reflected on the experience.

Finally, at the end of her essay, Abby shares her **message**:

I am a person who wants to reach out to and connect with all kinds of people.

What's interesting is that just about any story can be shaped to work within the parameters of a Common App essay, because how you think and write about your experience—rather than what merely happened—is what turns anecdote into essay. This can be seen in our next sample written by Jackson, an independent and confident student who decided he was a Hero: a resilient, ambitious crusader who takes courageous, difficult action to improve the world and prove his worth. Jackson's essay is ostensibly about building a set of rock steps. But as you'll see, it's really about so much more.

Jackson's Common App Essay

In the Allegheny National Forest on a remote section of the North Country National Scenic Trail, there is a set of eight steps that descend to the shallow crossing of a nameless stream. I built those steps.

Last summer I lived and volunteered for a month for the National Forest Service in Northwestern Pennsylvania. By chance I was chosen to work, with nine other strangers, on a

41

secluded trail in the Allegheny National Forest. The section was an absolute mess when we arrived, the trail itself being an overgrown, rutted, root-filled, eroded, steep, and generally unsafe travesty of trail-building and maintenance. Since the strategy that we adopted in an attempt to fix these problems was to divide and conquer, I found myself in a group of three tasked to engineer and construct a stone staircase at a particularly steep part of the path directly above a stream. We hastily picked out ten aesthetically pleasing, reasonably sturdy rocks and began to tear up the hillside and place stones as we went, letting each stone lay on top of the previous one to stabilize it as a stepping surface. After nine hours of hard labor in the heat and crushing humidity, we stepped back to admire our creation.

The following day, the trail foreman, our boss, came by to inspect our work. He was immediately impressed with the beauty of the project; he was equally unimpressed by the structural integrity of the staircase. He proceeded to mercilessly rip each step out of the ground with one hand, tossing them into the streambed where they shattered into hundreds of irrevocable pieces as I visibly struggled to hold back my tears.

"Do it again. But this time do it right."

For our second attempt, instead of 40–60

pound rocks, we selected 350–500 pound behemoths. This meant that we had to spend approximately six hours per rock just to painstakingly roll them into place using three unwieldy iron levers called rock-bars. It took us nine days, nine hours a day, of impossibly strenuous labor to finally finish that staircase, but when we were done there was no way any mortal being, nor flood of any proportion, could dislodge a single one of those rocks. The trail foreman came back the next day and gave us the coveted seal of approval. I had never been more proud of anything in my entire life. Not even close.

Until that moment, I was ignorant of the true definition of excellence. I had long associated the word with functionality, and while it's true that for a thing to be excellent it has to be functional, excellence is something far beyond that. It is often characterized by a variety of factors, but in reality it is somewhat ineffable—hard to define beyond a feeling of accomplishment and finality one gets upon the attainment of it. It is a feeling that asserts the caliber of the achievement and affirms beyond reasonable doubt that this creation is indeed a work of excellence. By equating excellence and functionality, I had put a cap on my abilities. I believed that there was no point in putting more work in if in the end it was the same result. However, this change in perception—those eight rocks—taught me the real purpose of greatness and how to achieve it. No longer will I be able to accept passable as a substitute for distinction.

When I came home from Pennsylvania, some three weeks of hard work later, I began to pursue excellence obsessively. I read, I wrote, I practiced, I listened, and I studied. I was trying to build my next staircase, and I have no intention of stopping.

If you find yourself hiking the North Country Trail next spring and you come to a set of eight lonely steps leading to a stream crossing, walk them confidently; you're on solid ground.[6]

So, what did Jackson do right?

He told a story with a clear **beginning, middle, and ending** (he was tasked with building the stairs; he tried and failed; he tried again and succeeded) filled with **conflict** (after his boss ripped out the first set of steps, would Jackson fight back or bounce back?), **suspense** (would his boss approve the second set of steps?), and **passion**.

He wrote in his own **unique and confident voice**.

---

6   The building blocks of Jackson's essay:
Five Best-Day Words: ambitious, open minded, independent, disciplined, creative
Story: building stone steps to a stream in the wilderness
Message: The pursuit of excellence gives my life meaning.
Archetypes: Hero, Leader, Seeker

Just look at the precision in this sentence: *The section was an absolute mess when we arrived, the trail itself being an overgrown, rutted, root-filled, eroded, steep, and generally unsafe travesty of trail-building and maintenance.*

He **circled back.** After describing the steps in his opening paragraph when the reader doesn't understand their significance, he returned to them in his closing paragraph when the reader knows why the steps matter. Circling back in your closing to an element from your opening adds resonance and gives delight to the reader who is paying attention.

He broke up his 650 words of exposition with a single, powerful line of **dialogue**: *"Do it again. But this time do it right."* Boy, is that line impactful! Using dialogue allows you to break up your exposition and dramatize rather than just flatly describe your story. Dialogue is your friend, and showing is better than telling.

Jackson **varied the length of his sentences**, making them progressively shorter, thereby changing the rhythms and keeping the reader alert and engaged. He even had the nerve to end a paragraph with a fragment! As you read, compare the length of the first sentence here to the last: *It took us nine days, nine hours a day, of impossibly strenuous labor to finally finish that staircase, but when we were done there was no way any mortal being, nor flood of any proportion, could dislodge a single one of those rocks. The trail foreman came back the next day and gave us the coveted seal of approval. I had never been more proud of anything in my entire life. Not even close.*

Jackson used smart, wry **understatement** to create

humor when talking about his boss: *He was immediately impressed with the beauty of the project; he was equally unimpressed by the structural integrity of the staircase.*

He illustrated **how outrageously hard he's willing to work** to accomplish a goal.

He showed powerful **intellectual vitality:** how he takes what he learned in one part of his life (building the staircase) and carries it over to many parts of his life (reading, writing, practicing, listening, studying) . . . something every educator is thrilled to hear.

And he shared his message:

The pursuit of excellence—as I now understand it—

gives my life enormous meaning.

In Jackson's essay, we noted for the first time the effective use of dialogue. In the last of our three sample essays, let's pay attention to how Ella writes about engaging with a social movement sweeping the nation but manages to keep the essay focused on her own personal experiences.

Ella's Common App Essay

To feel a part of something bigger than yourself is one of the most empowering emotions ever. I experienced this when walking in a Black Lives Matter protest in New York City. While growing up in New York, I had never personally encountered blatant or violent racism like these victims of police brutality had, but I had experienced the long-term effect of micro-aggressions and interracial misunderstanding. So when I stood shoulder to shoulder with thousands of New Yorkers who looked nothing like me, I was filled with hope because my immediate community recognized the urgent call to all for social action.

My own call to action began years earlier as I made the transition from middle to high school. Before freshman year, I was only familiar with the Upper West Side and Harlem. So when I traveled a mere 3.7 miles to Chapin, my new school on the Upper East Side, I was stunned to encounter a completely foreign culture.

During the first weeks of school, I felt like an outsider amongst my new friends because of the color of my skin. In one conversation, we compared the small changes we'd have to make to our appearances to look more like actress Blake Lively, our image of physical perfection. One friend commented on changing the shape of her nose. Another mentioned lightening her eyes one shade of blue. Then I realized I must be the least beautiful of all because I would have to endure the most drastic changes. Over time, I observed my classmates' carefully constructed facades and materialistic mindsets and started to lose faith in the possibility of true friendships here. But I am not one to give up easily. By continuing to meet the girls with my innate curiosity and open mind, I eventually discovered our common humanity and formed authentic, gratifying, and invaluable relationships. I now recognize that going to Chapin was one of the most challenging and beneficial experiences of my life. It pushed me out of my comfort zone and strengthened my abilities as a student, friend, and leader.

Last summer I sought out an opportunity to pay forward these hard-earned skills as I helped develop and worked as a counselor at Fun and Friends, a camp for students of color, ages five through twelve, who attend private schools in New York City. The counselors—all private high school students of color—cultivated an environment where campers could see role models who looked like them.

As a counselor, I facilitated a lesson on education activist Malala Yousafzai. With the younger campers, we brainstormed traits we shared with Malala, and many kids walked away feeling more confident that they too possess leadership qualities. With the older campers, we explored Malala's perseverance in the face of violence and discussed oppression and gender inequality. It was incredibly rewarding to successfully create a safe space where campers made powerful connections between the struggles in Malala's life and the events and difficulties of their own.

After thirteen years of attending predominantly white private schools, I wish a program like Fun and Friends had been around when I was younger. Getting to know other kids at school who looked like me would have eased the small doubt I felt of whether or not I belonged in the classes I'd been a part of my entire childhood. And yet I can't help but feel grateful for the lessons I learned while facing these hardships, because they inspired me to persevere through tough situations, reach past differences to commonalities, and act on my deep passion for racial equality.

Bob Dylan once said, "Some people feel the rain, others just get wet." When it comes to the painful obstacles I will face in my life, I'm determined not to feel that rain. Rather, I will only allow it to get me wet as I work to help my community survive, thrive, and grow.[7]

---

7 The building blocks of Ella's essay:
Five Best-Day Words: charismatic, hardworking, understanding, funny, contemplative
Story: working at camp for younger students of color to help them feel empowered and included
Message: I work to help my community survive, thrive, and grow.
Archetypes: Caregiver, Leader
Note: Because this essay doesn't show her funny side, Ella decided to share that part of herself in some of her supplemental essays. Remember, not every essay will share every side of you. That's why you should consider supplemental essays as wonderful opportunities to paint a fuller, more complete portrait of yourself.

What did Ella do well?

She decided her **archetypes** were the Caregiver and the Leader, so she looked for and found an experience that showed her in precisely that light.

She **grabbed her readers' attention** by opening with something philosophical (the power of being part of something larger than herself) and practical (standing shoulder to shoulder with other New Yorkers in a Black Lives Matter protest). This revealed her to be a thoughtful, active, and outward-looking young adult who **embraces the diversity** in the crowd.

Ella told an **authentic story** with a **beginning, middle, and ending** (she felt like an outsider as an African American student at a predominantly white school, spent years building bridges and meaningful connections with her peers, and then took the lessons she'd learned to a camp for younger students of color to inspire their pride, empowerment, and sense of belonging).

She described her **struggles** and vulnerability while facing social challenges at her new school, and she illustrated her **adaptability** and **resilience** when she refused to give up and ultimately forged sustaining friendships.

She revealed her unique **character, passion, and purpose**: when she sees an opportunity to nurture young people who feel disconnected, **she takes joyful, impactful action** to help them feel connected. And by **building a bridge** to younger students of color, she proved herself to be a **generous, giving community member**.

Ella avoided generalities and dove deep into **specifics**. Instead of just saying that she taught the campers about Malala, she wrote: *With the younger campers, we brainstormed traits we shared with Malala, and many kids walked away more confident that they too possess leadership qualities. With the older campers, we explored Malala's perseverance in the face of violence and discussed oppression and gender inequality.* Specifics bring a story to life and draw readers in.

Ella kept the **focus on herself**. She didn't let her essay become about her cause (racial and social justice). Instead, she shared the specific personal experiences that hooked her on her cause and the concrete actions she took to make a difference, revealing how she **grew** and **changed** along the way.

At the end of her essay, she proudly declared her **message**:

I intend to work to help my community survive, thrive, and grow.

CHAPTER 4

HOW TO FIND YOUR TOPIC

If you're like most students, you might not know right away what to write about. So I'm going to offer you several different ways to brainstorm and find your topic.

Story Prompts

The first and most common way to find a story is to ask questions. Lots of questions! When I worked with Abby, the girl who wrote about the corn maze, she knew she felt like an Adventurer, but she couldn't find the right story to tell because she was looking for a *big huge life-changing experience,* and like most seventeen-year-olds, she just hadn't had a lot of *big huge life-changing experiences.* It wasn't until I asked her dozens of questions that she finally got the idea to write about the corn maze. Do you know what question I asked that got her there? I said, "Abby, tell me about the most joyous moment of high school you can remember." And then she thought of standing on top of the haystack and how electric she felt.

After she told me the story, she said, "Oh, but I can't write about that. It was just a Halloween night. It wasn't significant." But it was hugely significant for her. We just had to tease out the message so the admissions officers would understand why it mattered.

For some students, thinking about their best and most joyful moments reminds them of an impactful, rewarding, moving, revealing, or inspiring experience that they can write about. For others, examining their worst and most terrifying, upsetting, disconcerting, or embarrassing moments reminds them of a struggle they went through and how they ultimately overcame it. In both cases, the emotional stakes are wonderfully high.

Remember those word lists you wrote when we first began? Pull them out now and take a look. Do your Best Day Words trigger memories of specific, meaningful experiences? Do your Worst Day Words take you back to a difficult challenge? Contemplate both possibilities and see where they lead you. And if you're still looking for help in brainstorming, here are the questions I ask my students as they search for their stories.

Questions to Help You Find Your Story

What qualities do you possess and how do they change the way you live?[8]

What places have you visited and why are they significant to you?

What single, unexpected object holds great meaning for you and why?

---

8 Need some ideas to get started? How about these: drive, humor, generosity of spirit, creativity, an analytic and inquisitive way of thinking, loyalty, optimism, boldness, fearlessness, honor, strength, flexibility, adaptability, dependability, tentativeness, stubbornness, introversion, cautiousness, discipline, work ethic, tenaciousness, sensitivity, blind faith, steadfastness, etc.

What relationship has been the most important to
   you and why?

Is there someone who has shifted your point of view?

Under what circumstances do you learn best?

What really fascinates you?

What have you discovered in life?

What is the funniest thing that's happened to you?

When have you felt rage?

When have you felt pride?

When have you felt hope?

When have you felt most connected to other people?

When have you felt most connected to nature?

What is the most joyous moment you can remember?

What is the darkest moment you can remember?

What is your biggest fear?

What activities are you most proud of participating in,
   and how has participating in them changed you?

What big idea, motto, catchphrase, or mantra has
   colored the way you live your life?

When did you change in an unexpected way?

What is something you used to believe and don't believe anymore?

What is something you thought was true but turned out to be false?

What have you had a change of heart about?

What have you been willing to fight for?

What would you be willing to fight for?

What has been your most ambitious goal and did you achieve it?

What has been your greatest struggle and how did you overcome it?

What has been your biggest disappointment and how did you recover?

What is the most terrifying/upsetting/disconcerting/ embarrassing moment you can remember, and how did you respond?

What have you failed at and what did you learn from that experience?

When have you not given your all and regretted it, and how did that change you?

When did your feelings for a friend or family member change, what caused that shift, and what did you learn about yourself?

What has been your most meaningful
   accomplishment?

What do people not know about you?

What have you done that everyone said you couldn't do?

If your life passed before your eyes, what moment
   would jump out at you?

When you lie awake in the middle of the night, what
   do you think about?

What motivates and drives you?

As you ask these questions, rummaging through past experiences and searching for potential messages, make notes of everything that pops into your head. Then examine your notes with a critical eye and the goal of digging deeper. Analyze your responses and ask yourself further questions:

Were these experiences significant? Why?

Did any of these experiences change you or the way you
   live or think? How?

What did you learn about yourself? About others?
   About life?

Do you see a pattern emerging?

Do you see particular values or concerns emerging?

Do those values and concerns define and reveal who
   you are?

Take some time to give all your ideas a chance to develop. As you ruminate, see if there is a valuable story and message there. Ultimately, does one experience begin to stand out? Does it carry your message and show who you authentically are?

If you find yourself wrestling with ideas for several viable stories and you are having trouble choosing, know that there is no right or wrong in this process. Discuss your choices with a trusted friend, then go with the one you instinctively feel best illustrates your best qualities. If you do, no matter which one you choose, you can't go wrong. (And don't forget that you might be able to use the leftover stories in your supplemental essays!)

Finally, understand that even if you write your essay about your experience on a soccer team or in the French Club, at summer camp or an afterschool job, it's not really about soccer or the French Club or your summer camp or an afterschool job. It's about you. Each of those arenas is merely a setting in which you met challenges, struggled, grew, and gained new understanding.[9]

Big Impacts

Have you ever made a snap judgment about someone only to discover later that you were wrong? I love when that happens. And lucky for me, given that my work entails sitting down with complete strangers on a daily basis and talking

---

9 This idea of keeping your essay focused on yourself is particularly important if you choose to write about the death of someone you cared for. Writing about a death can be a risky endeavor, as it's easy to fall into the trap of writing about the person who died rather than writing about yourself. If you do decide to write about a death, make sure you spend most of the essay illustrating how the lessons you learned from that person changed your perspective, colored the way you live your life, and led you to take concrete action.

for hours until we uncover the very thing that makes them unique, it happens to me a lot.

One summer, I was sitting across the dining room table from a student named Molly, who considered herself a Seeker. Like so many of the young people I meet, she was a hardworking, dedicated, disciplined student. At first, that's all I could see. We talked about her academics, her twelve years of athletics, her community service. She'd done everything right. From the outside, she seemed perfect and—though I hate to admit it—perfectly ordinary.

Just as I began to worry that we might not find anything unique and meaningful for her to write about, she made a passing reference to quitting her club swim team. "Why'd you do that?" I asked. And that's when she surprised me.

"Because I read a book that inspired me to make a change."

Okay, if I was curious before, I was captivated now. The conversation that ensued led Molly to write the following essay.

Molly's Common App Essay

My hands grip the edge of the block. The beeper sounds, and I explode off. After a streamlined glide, I rise to the surface, each stroke as automatic as a breath.

For most of my life, the swim club was my world. The pool was where I found friendship, developed confidence, and learned the undeniable power of brutally hard work.

During high school, I became one of the fastest sprinters in my group. As a sophomore, I competed on a relay in the NCSA Junior Nationals in Florida. I had never felt more accomplished in my life.

Shortly after this thrilling experience, my prospects came to a sudden and unexpected halt. The sets I could normally do with ease left me gasping for breath and stopping at every wall. I underwent numerous tests, but the results perplexed my doctors. Even though practice only brought me pain and frustration, I still attended every day.

Yet my aspiration did not waver. I could picture myself overcoming this condition and jumping right back in where I left off. Amazingly, after a year of struggling, this finally happened. The doctors discovered I had a condition in which my vocal cords constricted and inhibited airflow. I was put on medication and my symptoms abated. In a high school swim meet, I swam a personal best in the 50-freestyle and broke the school record. I was back and should have been elated, but to my surprise, I wasn't.

Instead of eagerly jumping out of bed to swim, the alarm for my 5 a.m. practice brought me to tears. Instead of flying through the water, I now trudged through meets and practices feeling anxious and numb. No matter how fast I went, I did not feel fulfilled. Confused, I reminded myself: I am a swimmer; this is how I earn success. But then a different, more unsettling question crept into my mind: If I am not a swimmer, who am I?

In the midst of this crisis, my English class read and discussed Henry David Thoreau's *Walden*. I became fascinated by Thoreau's ideas on deliberate living. I examined my own life and realized I was not living with intention. My efforts, no matter how astounding, were meaningless because they were no longer making me happy. The lines, "Not till we are lost, in other words not till we have lost the world, do we begin to find ourselves . . ." were an awakening to me. I knew it was time to lose the world of competitive swim and abandon my outdated identity in search of a new, true self. So I finished the season and took a giant leap of faith: I quit the swim club.

Released from the restraints swimming had placed on me, I felt wonderfully free. I stopped living like a machine and started living with curiosity and an open heart. Over the summer, I happily gave my full effort to volunteering as a counselor at an animal shelter day camp. Senior year, I challenged myself in difficult classes and achieved more than I ever thought possible.

Most importantly, I spent time with the people I love. My relationships with close friends and family deepened immensely. I cherished the long conversations with my dad and silly jokes with my sister and no longer took those moments for granted.

Looking back on my experience as a swimmer, I feel proud of all that I accomplished. But ironically, the lesson I feel most grateful for is what I learned from quitting swim: that sometimes the only way to evolve into our new selves is to step away from the old world that has defined us. Having done it once, I know I won't ever be afraid to do it again.[10]

My original assessment that Molly was ordinary could not have been more wrong. Here's a girl who thinks and feels deeply and has the courage to take chances and make unexpected changes in her life when all the pressures around her are telling her to stay the course. In recounting this story, Molly won my admiration.

She also taught me an incredibly important lesson. Now, whenever I help a student brainstorm essay ideas, I

---

10 The building blocks of Molly's essay:
Five Best-Day Words: happy, funny, passionate, kind, caring
Story: quitting club swim team
Message: To live with intention and authenticity in the present, I must be willing to walk away from what has defined me in the past.
Archetypes: Dreamer, Caregiver

always ask what the student's influences are: favorite novels, poems, music, lyrics, photographs, films, pieces of art, quotes, philosophies, news sources, blogs, podcasts, YouTube channels, moments in history? Favorite writers, athletes, leaders, composers, scientists? Favorite subject in school? Favorite piece of literature, fiction or nonfiction? As I ask these questions, I listen for what's had a big impact on the way a student lives or thinks.

If you can think of something that's had an impact on you, like *Walden* had on Molly, you might find a great essay in exploring how it relates to/resonates in/affects your life. Understand that you will still have to share a story about yourself, with a **beginning, middle, and ending,** but the external catalyst for change—no matter how unexpected—might help you frame the experience and articulate your message. In Molly's case, her **message** was this:

> To live with intention and authenticity in the present I've learned I must be willing to walk away from what has defined me in the past.

I like to call this kind of essay a **Big Impact** essay because it explores how something you encountered or learned altered the trajectory of your life. Here are some of my students' Big Impacts that made for great essays:

* A student was so inspired by the pro-individualism perspective of a novel's main character that it caused her to reassess her high school's pro-conformity social scene. (She was reacting to

Randle Patrick McMurphy in *One Flew over the Cuckoo's Nest* by Ken Kesey.)

* Another student explored her experience volunteering with disabled teens through the lens of a contemporary philosopher's call for society to stop marginalizing the disabled. (She had read about Jean Vanier's international federation, the Ark.)

* A third student critically examined his personal values and actions while seeking inner peace at a Buddhist meditation retreat and then went home to make real and positive changes in his life.

* And a fourth was so moved by a novel's star-crossed lovers who declared their love for one another despite their society's disapproval that it inspired her to break free from her parents' expectations and study acting. (Her change of heart was due to Elizabeth and Darcy in Jane Austen's *Pride and Prejudice*.)

Being open to impact and having the ability to connect what you learn to how you live is one of the most exciting qualities a school can see in you. So find something you've learned, read, or seen, and share how it changed the way you live.

A Unique Point of View

When my son, Sam, was born, he emerged with a big, round head and giant ears. My husband instantly fell in love with those ears and wrote odes to them, waxing poetic about the wonderful things Sam would hear with them. Little did we know at the time how prophetic those poems would be.

You see, Sam was born with perfect pitch. That means that any note he hears, he can name. After starting piano lessons at five, he would walk down the street, hear a car horn honk, and happily announce, "E flat!" At six, he could listen to a simple song and play it back on the piano. At seven, he went through a Beatles phase. At eight, it was ragtime, and one day he walked into a music store, stepped up to an unfamiliar harp, and immediately began plucking out "Boogie Woogie Bugle Boy" on the strings. At nine, he was composing his own music. At ten, he could spontaneously transpose from one key to another. At eleven, he started studying and improvising jazz. Now, at thirteen, if Sam is in a room with a piano, he literally cannot keep his hands off it. All his life, it's as if Sam hears in color while the rest of us hear in black in white.

My son's musical gift has changed the way he experiences the world. He constantly hears rhythms and music in his surroundings and in his head (yes, he was the kid on the soccer field whose fingers were always wiggling at his side, playing invisible keyboards as he waited for the ball to come near). And he notices things the rest of us miss ("Mom, pop songs are so annoying because they all use the same four chords over and over. Boring!")

Sometimes in life, a person's point of view is deeply affected by a particular sensitivity, fascination, passion, experience, or intention. In Sam's case, it's his sensitivity to sound and music. Everything he hears sparks his curiosity and alters how he feels, what he thinks, who he is drawn to, and how he lives. When it comes time for Sam to write his Common App essay, I'll be surprised if he doesn't choose to write about his uniquely musical point of view.

If you are a person who looks at the world through a particular lens, be it fashion or the environment or irreverent comedy or social justice or numbers or food, that lens might lead you to a **Unique Point of View** essay. I once sat down with a student named Josh to help him brainstorm his essay. When I asked what he might want to write about, he surprised me when he said, "Doing good." Curious, I asked what he meant. He then shared that he has a father who does harm wherever he goes, so Josh has committed himself to doing good wherever he goes. I asked if he could illustrate that unique point of view and sense of purpose with specific examples from his life. Here's what he wrote:

Josh's Common App Essay

There once was a father who committed heinous crimes and was sentenced to life in prison. He had two sons, one who was a model citizen, and one who became a criminal. A reporter doing a story on the father interviewed the sons and asked them the same question, "What made you the person that you are?" Both sons had the exact same reply: "With a father like that, what else could I be?"

My father is a very difficult person who almost never takes responsibility for his actions. He is not honest or ethical, blames others no matter the circumstance, manipulates, and always puts himself first. After tirelessly attempting to remedy my father's faults for years, I finally saw the devastating truth that he was not going to change. So I turned my focus away from him and asked myself, "Who am I?" "What do I value?" and "What kind of person do I want to be?" A clear answer reverberated through me: I will be everything my father is not, and everywhere I go I will try to do good.

Sophomore year, as I prepared for my chemistry final, I spent many hours creating a ten-page practice test. When I saw how effectively it helped me master the year's content, I happily shared the test with my entire grade because I thought it could help everyone succeed. Following this, I was thrilled to notice a more collaborative climate grow throughout the class.

I have always loved sports. Throughout high school, I've played on three varsity teams and been named MVP of my baseball team twice. Junior year, I wanted to share this passion with my school and give everyone an opportunity to play, regardless of experience, so I started Sports Club. I filled our weekly meetings with fun games and enabled many students to be on a team for their first time. By the end of the year, my club proudly held the highest attendance in the school.

Outside of school, I wanted to continue to do good, so I joined the San Francisco boys chapter of BBYO, an international Jewish youth group committed to improving the lives of others. While there, I recognized problems that I wanted to solve, so I ran and became chapter president. At our events, I noticed a segregation of friend groups and some isolated individuals. This was of paramount concern to me because BBYO was supposed to be a welcoming place where everyone could come together as one. To overcome this challenge, I restructured our events to mix groups and stress teamwork. Soon, everyone felt more included, and new friendships were kindled.

Looking for an opportunity to have an even greater impact, I applied for and earned a summer internship at a small employment law firm that helps people who do not receive fair wages or who experience harassment or discrimination in the workplace. In my two summers at the firm, I analyzed underpaid hours and screened and interviewed potential clients. I even helped a partner by doing ten hours of critical data calculations over one weekend though he never asked me to. I loved giving a voice to the voiceless and experiencing the power of doing for others.

Every morning, I wake up and think about the harm my father has done. So each day I get out of bed and work to repair it by doing as much good as I possibly can. Having the dad I have has been a trial by fire, but it has taught me to assert myself in the face of bullying; live every day with honesty, integrity, generosity, and kindness; and dedicate myself to working hard not only for myself but also to benefit others.

Someday in the future, I might get asked the question "What made you the person that you are?" I hope to be able to answer simply: "I did."[11]

Josh could have chosen to write his entire essay about being an academic leader, a star athlete, a youth group president, or a law firm intern. Instead, he used those as illustrations of the most important theme in his life: doing good. Josh's unique point of view—his pursuit of goodness—is about more than what he does. It is about why he does what he does.

---

11 The building blocks of Josh's essay:
Five Best-Day Words: thoughtful, ambitious, committed, optimistic, generous
Story: doing good in all parts of his life
Message: Everywhere I go, I try to do good.
Archetypes: Seeker, Leader

If you have a specific point of view, like Josh's, exploring it can be a great way to find and launch your essay. In Josh's case, he told one colorful, lively, multifaceted story about pursuing goodness. Along the way, he beautifully illustrated his five words that best describe him on his best day: thoughtful, ambitious, committed, optimistic, generous. He used his Seeker and Leader archetypes to help him articulate his message:

Everywhere I go, I try to do good.

And there's one more thing Josh did particularly well that we can all learn from. Josh planted an idea in his opening (the parable of the father who does evil and the sons who use his example as an inspiration to do good or an excuse to do evil). At first, the reader just thinks he is telling the parable to set up the themes of fatherhood, good, and evil. But when Josh reaches his closing, he circles back to the parable and poses the central question to himself: "What made you the person that you are?" Josh answers, "I hope to be able to answer simply: I did."

By revisiting the parable, Josh makes it relevant to his own life and uses his answer to move his reader. It is a bold, impactful essay.[12]

Accentuate the Positive

My mom loves to listen to music, especially songs from the 1940s and '50s. Throughout my childhood, she often tuned

---

12 For another example of a Unique Point of View essay, see appendix B for Zianna's story about her passion for exploring the world.

the radio to play classics by crooners and torch singers like Louis Armstrong, Joe Williams, Ella Fitzgerald, Lena Horne, and Billie Holiday. One Saturday afternoon, I heard the lyrics of a jaunty, unfamiliar song that soon became my favorite: "You've got to accentuate the positive, eliminate the negative, latch on to the affirmative, don't mess with Mr. In-Between."[13] For students with less than stellar transcripts who are writing Common App essays, these words could not be truer.

By the time you apply to college, there's not much you can do to fix weak grades and low test scores. But when it comes to your essay, there is still room to support your cause. I learned this lesson while working with Cole, a student I like to describe as "average grades, above-average guy." When Cole and I sat down together, it immediately became clear that his merely passing grades would not be the thing to sell him to colleges. But after chatting and listening to him describe his life, I was blown away by his humor, personality, energy, and incredible willingness to work hard when he's engaged in something. In fact, if I could bet on the future success of only one of my students, I'd bet on him.

So if you're a student like Cole, whose grades and scores might not entice many colleges, how do you strategically use your essay to convince them to give you a chance? By telling a story that shares what you are good at. Examine your life and look for areas where you've found success. Are you

---

13 Music by Harold Arlen, lyrics by Johnny Mercer. Published in 1944.

great at rallying crowds? Unifying diverse people? Building things with your hands? Helping kids? Connecting with elderly people? Rescuing dogs? In Cole's case, he was great at keeping a positive attitude and bringing that attitude and willingness to work hard to the things he loves. Take a look at Cole's essay. After reading it you'll understand why, despite his unimpressive GPA, he was accepted at eight different colleges.

Cole's Common App Essay

I am cruising down the freeway in the green '71 Nova I just bought with my entire life's savings when I hear a loud pop followed by banging. Right off, I know my tire has blown. Though I have not had the Nova for long, she is not lovin' me tonight.

When the tow truck arrives, the Hispanic driver sees my car and smiles from ear to ear.

"Oh man, is that a Nova?"

I nod and smile back.

"My cousin had the same exact car, same exact color."

As he opens my trunk to check the spare tire, a huge smile spreads across his face.

"It smells like my childhood."

As the driver tows me, he laughs as he explains that in Spanish "no va" means "no go," and then I get his entire life story. As he reminisces, I see how a small thing like my car can take someone back to such a happy time.

Before the driver leaves, he tells me I made his day, and I tell him he made mine as well. Just like that, a terrible night turns into one I will never forget. And I realize that all it takes is a good attitude.

Not long after that night, I work my first shift at a little pizza joint called Tonino's Place. When I arrive, I expect the owner to hand me a manual. Instead, she says, "Make yourself busy!" So I do. I throw on an apron, scrub a mountain of pots and pans and get soaking wet in the process. I teach myself how to bus tables, clean windows, and pack to-go orders. Then I get very good at loading and unloading the dishwasher.

Over time, I come to love my job because there is always something to do or something new to learn. Sometimes when I have a moment, I get Mario, the pizza chef, to teach me how to knead the dough. If Yuri, the cashier, feels lazy, I take over and learn how to ring up customers. When the time comes to deliver pizzas, I pack the bags, load the address into my GPS, and away I go. No matter how much I enjoy working in rhythm with the team in the kitchen, nothing tops the feeling of handing someone a hot pizza after they've had an obviously tough day.

At the end of each shift, I put the chairs up, sweep, and mop. The toughest part of my shift comes last: the trash. I take a deep breath and hold it, carry three giant bags into the alley, open the Dumpster filled with rotting meat, and fling the bags in.

It's true that my job is not glamorous, and the average person might think it stinks. But I love it. Because during every single shift, I turn something bad into something good and make every situation fun for everyone.

When I go to college, I know I won't arrive with 4.0 GPA. But I will arrive with other valuable qualities. If I walk into a room full of strangers, I can talk to anyone and make friends with everyone. Of the roughly 700 kids in my graduating class, I can say with supreme confidence that I can name ninety percent of them. When I have a job to get done, I give it my all. I am capable and curious, smart and motivated.

For as long as I can remember, my classes and goals have been assigned by the adults in my life. But college will be my chance to choose my own classes and goals based on my real interests and passions. I can't wait to work hard, make the most of my time and abilities, and pursue the knowledge and ambitions that matter to me. With my positive attitude, I know I will take the world by storm.[14]

---

14 The building blocks of Cole's essay:
Five Best-Day Words: warm, funny, smart, outgoing, caring
Story: working at a pizza joint
Message: I am capable, curious, and motivated, and my positive attitude will help me take the world by storm.
Archetypes: Caregiver, Artist, Leader

Cole's essay succeeds because he found a story that accentuates the positive and paints a clear picture of how he will contribute to his future college community. If you are an average or below-average student whose appeal isn't obvious, think about the very real ways you have enlivened your community, and then find a story that shows you making the most of an opportunity and contributing in your own unique way.[15]

Intellectual Vitality

If you find yourself on the high end of the academic achievement spectrum, you might want to illustrate how you use your mind to discover and create new connections and make the most of opportunities in and out of the classroom. One of the best examples I've ever seen of this was a student who went to Spain for a summer language-immersion program. When she found out her classes were scheduled only during the morning, she started looking for a way to fill her afternoons. Following much investigation, she came up with the idea to do an independent research project on the faltering Spanish economy in the context of a struggling EU community. After studying complex economic terminology—in Spanish, no less!—she got in touch with a local professor who agreed to let her interview him. After their ninety-minute meeting, she then joined three generations of

---

15 If you're interested in reading another essay about an afterschool job that was written by a very different kind of student, check out Fiona's essay in appendix C. It's by a bright, thoughtful, highly accomplished student who gets a job at Starbucks and learns not to make assumptions about people on either side of the counter.

his family for lunch, where they further debated the topics from many diverse points of view. On that afternoon, while discussing complex ideas in a foreign language with virtual strangers, she had never been happier or felt more alive. In telling this story, the student illustrated how she bravely follows her curiosity and takes initiative in unique ways to learn as much as possible. And she infused her essay with emotion and humanity by tying her curiosity about the world to the fact that she is the daughter of an immigrant.

To read an essay by another intellectually ambitious student, take a look at Nathan's. As you'll see, illustrating his intellectual nimbleness was no problem for Nathan. What was more challenging was finding a way to make the essay not only brainy but also emotional. He chose to use his relationship with his grandfather to frame the essay to great effect.

Nathan's Common App Essay

When I was nine years old, I stole my first book. Lucky for me, I wasn't punished. Instead, I was encouraged.

The book, *Tristes Tropiques* by Lévi-Strauss, came from the library of my Parisian grandfather— my mom's dad—an accomplished psychoanalyst. Because my father has long been absent from my life, it was my grandfather who taught me to push myself intellectually, think critically, follow my curiosity, and enthusiastically explore art and culture in all forms. By the time I was twelve, we were having conversations about Heidegger, Nietzsche, and Foucault. When I was thirteen, he dared me to read Jung and Steiner. By fourteen, I spoke four languages while trying to catch up to his six. Throughout my childhood, my grandfather's passions inspired my own and launched me on a journey of investigation, discovery, and learning.

While attending high school in Paris, I read Nabokov's *Lolita*. The book astonished me. The prose was poetic and enchanting, dark and curious, and soon after I decided to attend a conference titled "Nabokov and Happiness." While there, I met a writer who was preparing a night dedicated to Jean-Paul Sartre. When I asked if I could attend, she thrilled me with an offer to be her assistant. On that day, from 7 a.m. to midnight, I worked tirelessly, learned vast amounts about Sartre, and even explored the themes of existentialism in the life of a teenager. Later in the week, over a Chinese tisane, I told my grandfather about the great minds I had encountered, from a Nobel laureate quantum physicist to an illustrious writer who had mingled with Derrida and Foucault in his twenties.

During one of my adventures in the great bookstores of Paris, I came upon *Birth of a Theorem*. Intrigued by the jacket photo of the peculiar author dressed as a magician, I decided to immerse myself in the universe of mathematics. The wizard was Cédric Villani, the Fields Medal recipient for advancements in the study of the mathematical properties of gas expansion. Inspired by the work, I wrote the author and asked if we could meet. To my great surprise, Mr. Villani agreed. Before this encounter, I was nervous, as I'd never found mathematics as intellectually liberating as literature or philosophy. However, the unconditional curiosity that my grandfather had transmitted to me brought me back to a Zen state; in the middle of our conversation's whirlwind of ideas and concepts, I was at home.

Not long after I met Villani, my mother, younger sister, and I moved to Los Angeles for my mother's work. The hardest part was leaving my grandfather behind. As I rode my bike across this fascinating, multicultural city, I happened upon bookstores and dove into English-language books. One day, while reading *Surely You're Joking, Mr. Feynman!*, the autobiography of physicist Richard Feynman, I was interrupted by the phone ringing downstairs. It was my grandfather in tears.

My grandfather was suffering from arrhythmia and needed immediate heart surgery. Because I was 5,659 miles away, the only support I could offer was to talk, and boy, did we talk! Like in the good old days, we discussed everything: my latest reads about quantum physics, his new Italian *recettes*, the state of the world, my impressions of my new home.

As soon as I could, I flew back to Paris to help him recover and to care for him as he had always cared for me. I felt lucky to be able to express my gratitude to him for inspiring my curiosity, pushing me to challenge myself in every way, and enticing me to view each moment as an opportunity to learn.

After two weeks, my grandfather was doing well and I had to fly home. Once again, we said our goodbyes, and I returned to Los Angeles. But not, I must confess, without leaving a few new empty spaces in his library.[16]

If knowledge is what propels you to action, you too might have an **intellectual vitality** story to share. Just make sure you find a personal way into your story so your reader can be moved by your mind *and* heart.

---

16 The building blocks of Nathan's essay:
Five Best-Day Words: adventurous, curious, energetic, musical, passionate
Story: how his grandfather sparked his intellectual curiosity and Nathan ran with it
Message: Every day I passionately seek out new ideas and unfamiliar ways of thinking.
Archetypes: Seeker, Adventurer, Artist
Circling Back: He opened the essay with his grandfather's library and circled back to that library in his closing.

Learning Differences

Throughout time, some people have had learning differences that made it difficult for them to absorb information in typical ways. Too often these individuals were made to feel stupid and incapable. Lucky for us, today those with learning differences can get them diagnosed so they understand their brains' strengths and challenges and learn viable work-arounds.

If you are a student with learning differences, you might not look like the typical college applicant. So how do you get schools to appreciate what you offer? My students Brian and Siena exemplify two varied approaches.

When I sat down with Brian, who has dyslexia, he said, "You cannot know who I am without knowing the struggles I've faced in school and how hard I've worked to overcome them." He insisted he write directly about how dyslexia had shaped his young life.

When Siena walked into my office, she said, "Yeah, sure, I have dyslexia, ADD, and auditory processing disorder, but those are the least interesting things about me!" Siena knew that her learning differences would be documented on her transcript, and she didn't want to even mention them in her essay. She instead wanted to use her essay to show who she is when you meet her outside the classroom in the larger world: a fearless, creative, exceptionally capable young woman.

If learning differences are something you wrestle with, take a look at these very different but equally impactful essays. And know that the best way to advocate for yourself is to put yourself at a college or university that understands students with learning differences and is committed to offering them the support they need to succeed.

Brian's Common App Essay

It is a sunny afternoon after school in third grade and my triplet brothers and I rush to finish our homework so we can play outside. After quickly reading a two-page story, my brothers are up and out the door. But I am still staring at the paper, frustrated that I have only finished half a page while they are both done. I know I am as smart as my brothers, so why can't I read like them?

I am dyslexic. In my case, that means that when I read I add suffixes and prefixes, see words that are not there, mistake one word for another, and move at a terribly slow pace. After two tests confirmed my diagnosis, I was sent to a special education school to improve my reading. In the beginning, it was odd to be away from my brothers. The new school had only eight kids in my grade for one-on-one training. Given that the only way to overcome dyslexia is to read, the school got me reading all the time.

Because my skills improved, in seventh grade I was able to transfer to a slightly larger special ed school. I continued to work hard, and even though my reading skills were lower than a typical reader, my higher-level thinking moved me into the top sections for math, English, history, and science. Looking ahead to high school, I realized that I wanted to be in school with my brothers again, so I got to work and read independently for practice. Months later, when Loyola High School sent out their acceptance letters, I was thrilled that all three of us got in.

The fall I started at Loyola was the first year the school accepted students with dyslexia. I was one of the first and wanted to prove I could handle it. Loyola was different from my previous schools. My grade had 330 students and the school assigned a ton of reading, lots of essays, and long papers to be written under quick deadlines. It was a huge challenge, but I worked twice as hard as everyone else, and I succeeded, slowly improving my grades every semester. After spending years separated from my brothers, it was great to be back in school with them, allowing us to support each other, take classes together, and share friends.

My brain works differently than other people's. For most people, you can present a problem and a solution and their brain accepts it. But if you present my brain with a problem, it insists on approaching it from every angle, seeking all possible solutions, and looking for alternate routes before it can settle down and accept the right answer. In school, this can be challenging because my brain jumps through more hoops and takes longer to process information. But in the real world, this can actually be a positive. This has been the case in computer programming. I have taught myself to create strategy and action games that I find interesting and fun. When I face coding problems and obstacles, I approach them in multiple ways. I sit and focus deeply, seek out resources, build syntax, and experiment for hours on end, never giving up.

Dyslexia is one piece of my life. It is a challenge I must overcome, but it does not define who I am. I define myself by being an active member of my school's Programming Club and Investment Club, performing community service, and playing basketball and socializing with my friends. What is important is that I am making strides every day, and I am willing to work hard to support my growth. Through dealing with dyslexia, I have experienced the value of hard work, determination, resilience, and focus. I have learned what I am made of. And having accomplished all that I have makes me passionately believe that every goal I set is within my reach.[17]

---

17 The building blocks of Brian's essay:
Five Best-Day Words: kind, helpful, hardworking, creative, athletic
Story: overcoming dyslexia
Message: I take nothing for granted and work every day to support my own growth.
Archetypes: Seeker, Hero

Siena's Common App Essay

I have studied art history at Cambridge University, where I soaked up Rothko, Turner, and Abramovic. I have conducted interviews, written articles, and taken photographs for my school's online newspaper, challenging myself to take risks and ask questions. I have collaborated with peers to mount shows in my school's student-run gallery, curating exhibits, managing social media accounts, and happily sharing the art with my community. I have stood on a UCLA stage and performed the play I wrote about Andy Warhol's Factory girl Edie Sedgwick, deeply moved by her tragically flawed life. But the moment that made me feel most alive was standing in the bustling street of a foreign city, hair drenched with rain, body shivering with cold, feet sore in high heels, but hands filled with one giant, glorious, butcher-paper-wrapped bundle.

It is spring break of 2014, and I am a sixteen-year-old Los Angeles native embarking on a trip to Germany for an experience that will forever change my life: a two-week internship at the NPR Bureau in Berlin. My job there entails helping with the nitty-gritty of producing their first annual art auction gala fundraiser. I create computer spreadsheets, communicate with artists, and run to galleries all over the city to pick up pieces. On this day, my job is to track down a particular artist at his studio and solicit a donation of one of his works.

As I set off across the city, feeling confident on the outside but nervous on the inside, I become distracted by children playing in a park and stop to take photos. Just then, it starts to rain, and immediately I regret my choice of high heels and Southern California attire. Dashing back into the streets, I quickly become lost. I ask strangers for help, but they just laugh at my pronunciation.

Eventually, with a bit of luck, I locate the building I am looking for. I walk up six flights of stairs, find the studio, and knock. When a paint-spattered artist opens the door, he has absolutely no idea who I am or why I'm there. Quickly I explain myself, and miraculously he invites me in.

That's when the magic happens. As soon as I step inside, I am blown away by the graffiti-style urban art and messy colors that explode across the space. I am thrilled to see so much raw expression and can't take my eyes off the beautiful images he has created.

The artist and I talk, through his broken English and my nonexistent German, and I plead and cajole and campaign. At last, he agrees to donate a piece. A smile spreads across my face. The artist grabs a 4'×3' canvas, wraps it in brown butcher paper, and hands it to me. Amazed, I offer enormous thanks.

As I emerge onto the rainy street, I am glowing with excitement. I know this painting will move everyone who has the opportunity to see it, just like it moved me. I know the funds it raises at the auction will benefit the bureau in real ways. And I feel so proud to have accomplished my goal and done my part.

I am ambitious in life and passionate about the arts. Every day I actively look at and engage in the world around me. I think about characters and experiences and then create and share stories and images. I seek out real-world opportunities and responsibilities and see them through. When I encounter obstacles, I plow through them with joy, nerve, and curiosity. By studying art, photography, acting, writing, film, and journalism in college, I intend to further pursue beauty, great stories, and, most importantly, authentic truths.

Exploring the world. Going outside my comfort zone. Working with others to accomplish meaningful goals. Sharing what I discover. These will be the steps along my unique path to accomplish work of imagination and impact.[18]

---

18 The building blocks of Siena's essay:
Five Best-Day Words: creative, passionate, fearless, fun, capable
Story: internship in Berlin
Message: I pursue beauty, great stories, and truth with joy, nerve, and curiosity.
Archetypes: Artist, Hero, Adventurer

Creativity

If you are a sensitive, creative person, you might want the theme of your essay to relate to what you observe in the world and how you respond to it uniquely. But you can't just write in vague generalities. You must dig deep to find the specifics.

On one bright summer afternoon, I sat down to work with Annie at her family's kitchen table. She knew she felt most alive while being creative, but she had no idea what story to tell. So I posed lots of questions about her various artistic endeavors. Then I asked her to choose a project that engaged her abilities to observe and imagine, challenged her to go outside her comfort zone, made her innovate, and taught her an important lesson about herself and the act of creating. If your archetype is the Artist, I encourage you to read Annie's essay and then ask yourself these same rigorous questions.

Annie's Common App Essay

I have a history with perfectionism. In junior high, I strived to be as well rounded as I could possibly be. I followed the phrase "be the best version of yourself" too literally, leading to a ceaseless drive to be the perfect track star, volleyball stud, ballerina, scholar, friend, and artist. As soon as high school began, something inside me started to change. I loosened my grip on the pursuit of perfectionism and started to focus on activities that genuinely interested me, challenged me, and made me feel alive and present. I shed activities that I no longer felt connected to, which opened up free time and gave me the opportunity to learn about myself and my understanding of the world.

In eleventh grade, I took my first video production class. I knew nothing about making films and had little experience with telling stories through the moving image, but I was curious. On the first day, I learned the basics of lighting, sound, and mise-en-scène. As soon as I learned which button turned the camera on and off, I was launched.

My first videos followed the rules of traditional storytelling. They had a beginning, middle, and end; recognizable characters; and suspense building to revelation. They were literal representations of the world as I saw it.

As I gained experience and confidence, I realized that filmmaking doesn't have to be so literal. For my last assignment of the year, I was thrilled to be allowed to create anything I wanted and was eager to try something new and experimental. I started with a song and the idea to use compositions of people and objects in graceful motion. I wasn't sure where the video was going, but I had a strong feeling that I should trust my creative instincts and let them run their course. Everywhere I went, my camera came with me: a construction site, a dance studio, a birthday tea, in the car, to school. My purpose over those two weeks was to capture everyday movement that I found compelling. I filmed my dad diving, a ballerina leaping, bicyclists racing, a globe spinning, bubbles blowing, my dog's tail wagging. Each shot had the same visual line. I played with the images, fitting them together like pieces of a puzzle. Then, after fiddling around with effects and composition, I suddenly got the idea to stream the shots in reverse. The result was magical and instantly compelling. I was in awe.

With one small change, I transformed shots of common objects and motions into extraordinarily uncommon images with unexpected meaning. By freeing myself from the constraints of literal, narrative, linear storytelling, I allowed myself to explore and create visual poetry in which all assumptions about reality dissolved. Everything about life as we know it, even laws of nature, could be defied. I discovered that abstract visual experience leads to reflections on perspective and life's ever-changing essence. I realized that all my life I had been limiting my creativity by being more concerned with tactile perfectionism rather than the gripping concept. Artistically, I had been a painter who reproduced the world as I literally saw it. In video production, I could recreate the world as no one has ever seen it.

In the past year, I have learned a lot about myself. I am most moved to realize that I am a person who does not need an answer in every moment. I am not only comfortable with the unknown, but I welcome it because it is in these moments of uncertainty that I make the most unexpected and extraordinary discoveries. As I look ahead, I am excited by all there is to learn and explore. Although I might not yet know the exact direction in which life will lead me, I do know that—like a figure who can dive up or a dancer who can leap backward—the possibilities are limitless.[19]

Annie chose to explore her creativity at a four-year college. If you're planning to explore yours at an art/design/film/music school, make sure your personal statement establishes your **unique perspective**, illustrates your **work ethic**, and conveys your **passion**.[20]

---

19 The building blocks of Annie's essay:
Five Best-Day Words: creative, strong, sensitive, joyful, connected
Story: video production class and project
Message: I embrace uncertainty, because it opens me up to the greatest creative possibilities.
Archetypes: Artist, Seeker, Adventurer
20 For another excellent example of an essay that explores creativity, see Andreas's Common App essay in appendix D. He was a student applying to film school to study animation.

Think Outside the Box

Samuel was a student who knew he wanted to write his essay about an all-consuming hobby but was afraid the college admissions officers would deem it insubstantial. After some coaxing, I finally got him to confess his passion: fantasy football. Knowing nothing about it, I asked him to tell me about it in detail. Twenty minutes later, I was wowed by its outrageous complexity, swept up by Samuel's enthusiasm, and certain that the admissions officers would be too if he clearly articulated his love for the league and all the ways that participating challenged him. (I also texted my brother, an avid fantasy footballer, to get in on next season's action.)

Samuel's Common App Essay

Draft Day 2016: after a ten-month-long, grueling off-season filled with constant practice, exertion, and analysis done to achieve perfection, I anxiously step into the tense room where my new season's fate will be determined. No, I am not a football player, a coach, or a general manager for an NFL team; I am a fantasy football player.

Although my dedication to a fantasy sport may seem peculiar, the fierce competition, mind-boggling statistics, and powerful community that I have formed with my "league" of competitors are all very real. Every fall for four years, I have played in an ESPN-hosted fantasy football league with my nine best friends. As general manager of my team,

I spend fifty preseason hours researching all NFL players. I study the ESPN analysts' top 300 rankings, read articles on bleacherreport.com, and participate in mock drafts to practice strategies. After filling multiple binders with research, I create a prioritized list of players and plan for all sixteen rounds of my draft to end up with a twenty-player roster.

During the last week of the NFL preseason, my friends and I gather on a crisp morning to hold our fantasy draft. Usually, we are a loud and comic bunch. Today, we are all business. After picking numbers to determine our order, we face the draft board and take turns choosing players for our teams. During the first two rounds, I'm thrilled to get the players I want, but by the third round, every player left on my wish list has been drafted. Now I must think fast, improvise, and trust my research and instincts. With each choice, I hear the banter of my fellow league members, "You're on the clock . . . make a move . . . don't mess up!" After three years of losing, I know that the decisions I make now will determine if this year I finally become the champ.

Once the regular NFL season begins, our fantasy league is on. Each week, the commissioner of our league organizes our ten teams into five matches. Based on how our players do in real games, our teams are assigned or docked points for players' successes and failures, and winners and losers are determined. Every week after the Monday night games, I manage and rework my roster. When players get injured, I must improvise and get new ones through free agency or by trading with other teams. If starters are doing poorly but bench players are doing well, I must adapt and switch them out. If an older player unexpectedly retires midseason—yes, this happened to me!—I must do more research and replace the retiree with younger talent. Over four years, I've learned that in fantasy football—like in life—nothing ever goes the way you expect it to, everything can and does happen, how you respond to challenges determines how well you do, and the person who puts in the most work does the best.

During high school, I have played junior varsity baseball and varsity golf. I have also been a broadcaster for my school's football team, which has given me a deep understanding and admiration for the game. But as crazy as it sounds, I have learned the most from fantasy football. Playing fantasy football has taught me to prepare, work insanely hard, adapt, and then work even harder. I am proud to say these lessons have carried over to my academic work. After underperforming in my freshman and sophomore years of high school, I realized the only way to succeed was to get organized, dedicate myself to my studies, and give everything my full effort. So I did. Junior year, my grades improved, and senior year, they keep getting better.

As a high school student, athlete, and young entrepreneur, I love competition. I cannot wait to take my drive and hard-earned work ethic to college where I will strive to gain the knowledge and skills necessary to win.[21]

Though Samuel's choice of topic might be unusual, the qualities and skills he reveals are extremely pertinent to being a great college student: **focus, dedication, adaptability, and resilience**. If you have an outside-the-box story you'd like to tell, examine it rigorously and frame it to illustrate the meaningful physical, intellectual, creative, and/or social skills it has pushed you to develop. If you do your job well, your readers will learn what they need to know about you and enjoy an unexpected gust of fresh air![22]

*****

---

21 The building blocks of Samuel's essay:
Five Best-Day Words: fun, ambitious, social, athletic, motivated
Story: fantasy football league
Message: When I am passionate about something, absolutely nothing can stop me.
Archetypes: Rebel, Seeker, Hero
22 To see another Think Outside the Box essay, check out Amanda's essay in appendix E. Writing during a presidential election year, she decided to craft her essay in the form of an open letter to the presidential candidates.

However you choose to brainstorm and search for essay topics, remember that you will want to bounce between **your five words, stories, messages**, and **archetypes**. Does a particular archetype or message remind you of an experience? Does a significant experience illustrate a possible message? Do your five words lead you to an important theme/point of view? Has something you've learned changed the actions you take or choices you make? Ideally you want to bounce back and forth among all these possibilities until the most meaningful ones begin to rise and converge around a single story that reveals something about you that really matters.

I know this process can be difficult. And it's not uncommon for a student to feel stalled. If that happens to you, don't despair, and don't get overwhelmed. Instead, take practical action to help yourself. Find a friend, and talk to each other. Tell your friend the stories you're considering writing and the messages you want them to illustrate. Allow your friend to ask rigorous questions to fine-tune your story. Use your archetype to help clarify your message.

Finally, believe that whoever you are today, you are enough. You don't have to have cured cancer to have a worthwhile story to tell. And you don't have to have discovered the meaning of life to have a significant message. A small, simple truth learned during your life so far—and how it's changed the way you're living it—is enough.

CHAPTER 5

OUTLINING YOUR ESSAY

Structure, Structure, Structure!

Okay, so you've selected the **story** you want to tell and used your chosen **archetype** to help you articulate the **message** you intend to deliver. Great! Now you're ready to figure out the best way to structure your essay and where to spend your precious 650 words.

When you reach this step in your process, it's important to understand the difference between your personal story and your essay's structure.

* Your **story**—the event or experience you are writing about, what actually happened—can be broken down into a chronological **beginning**, **middle**, and **ending**.

* Your essay's **structure**—how you organize and share all of your material—will be broken down into an **opening**, **body**, and **closing**.

Let's unpack story and structure to understand the difference.

In your chronological story's **beginning**, a problem arose, a question was posed, or a challenge was accepted.

In the **middle**, there were conflicts/struggles/obstacles, attempted solutions, mistakes and failure, critical thinking and innovation, and new attempted solutions. In the **ending**, you arrived at a resolution: ultimately you either succeeded or failed at your task.

But your essay will include more than just your chronological story. It might also include background information. It will definitely include a thoughtful reflection, such as why this experience mattered to you, how it changed you, what you learned from it, or your message. You might aim to broaden its scope by including related quotes, literary references, or song lyrics (more on this later). And you might scramble the chronology to heighten suspense—think about movies that play with time, jumping forward and backward to better raise and reveal the stakes.

Because every story can be told in many different ways, how you choose to structure your essay (what you strategically include in your **opening**, **body**, and **closing**) allows for some creativity: Do you give your reader a key piece of information up front, unspool it as you go, or withhold it for a big reveal at the end? Do you open in the middle of your story with a juicy, unresolved, conflict-riddled, or heightened moment to grab your reader's attention (**opening**), then give the background of how you got to that moment/why it mattered to you/what you learned (**body**), and finally reveal what action you took or choice you made (**closing**)? There is no right or wrong approach. The possibilities are unlimited and the choice is yours, but the goal is always the same: to find the most riveting, impactful way to draw in your reader and share your story and message.

Three Sample Structures

To explore this, let's go back to some essays you're already familiar with. Each told a story with a chronological beginning, middle, and ending, but each one structured its opening, body, and closing slightly differently. Let's take a look.

Jackson's Structure: 647-Word Essay[23]

Opening (37 words):

Briefly and mysteriously describes the remote wilderness scene, establishes the existence of the steps, and states that he built them.

Body (364 words):

Tells the **story** of building the steps with a **beginning** (describing task at hand), **middle** (trying, failing, trying again), and **ending** (succeeding).

Closing (246 words):

Reflects on what he learned from this experience and declares his **message** (how it changed the way he lives his life).

---

23   Read Jackson's essay on page 41.

Molly's Structure: 646-Word Essay[24]

Opening (31 words):

Throws the reader into a vivid moment in the midst of her swim story: before a swim race starts, the beeper sounds, she dives into the water, she swims; this grabs the reader's attention without explanation.

Body (520 words):

Tells her whole **story** by going back in time to the **beginning** (she had always been a swimmer, was successful, then got sick, struggled, then got healthy and still struggled), **middle** (read Thoreau's *Walden* and it changed her perspective), and **ending** (she quit swim and lived a fuller, happier life).

Closing (95 words):

Reflects on what she learned, how it changed her, how she plans to live in her future; shares her **message** (to be able to live in the present she must be willing to leave behind what defined her in the past).

---

24   Read Molly's essay on page 58.

Cole's Structure: 645-Word Essay[25]

Opening (202 words):

Tells an extended anecdote about his car breaking down that teaches him that all he needs in life is a positive attitude.

Body (282 words):

Tells the **story** of working at the pizza place with a **beginning** (starting the job), **middle** (seeking out new responsibilities), and **ending** (reflecting on why he likes and values it).

Closing (161 words):

Reflects on his real-life, real-world strengths, looks ahead to college, and expresses his **message** (with his positive attitude, nothing can stop him).

Though there are an unlimited number of ways to organize your essay, most students end up with some version of the following:

* **The Opening:** approximately **50–200 words** used to dramatically pull your reader into your story, set up necessary background information and context, or ask a compelling question.

---

25   Read Cole's essay on page 71.

* **The Body:** approximately **250–500 words** used to tell the necessary background and/or plot of your story with vivid details, specific examples, conflict, obstacles, humor, suspense, ups and downs, attempts, failures, innovation, new attempts, dialogue, and resolution.

* **The Closing:** approximately **50–250 words** used to discover and articulate what you learned, the meaning of your story, declare your message, possibly circle back to an element in your opening, and perhaps turn from your past to your future.

These word budgets are not set in stone. In fact, if you examine the sample structures we just looked at, you will see how much variation there can be. They are just meant as general guides. Because each story is different, the way you use your word budgets will differ too. By offering you these parameters I am merely trying to give you a framework within which to begin, which is always better than swimming in chaos and words. And, if you prefer an even firmer framework, I often advise students to start outlining with the following word budgets: **100/400/150**. From there, you can adjust depending on your particular story.[26]

---

26 If you're concerned that following this structure will make every essay look alike, take a look at the sixteen sample essays in appendix A. With varied stories, messages, authors' voices, structures, and word budgets, each one offers a glimpse into a fresh and unique world, character, and experience. It's like romantic-comedy movies: you know the boy will meet the girl, lose the girl, and win back the girl. But it's the specific way these things happen that make it feel forever new and keep us coming back for more. (*Footnote 26 continued on next page.*)

I once worked with an imaginative girl named Liv who came up with a great story to tell and then sat down and wrote a phenomenal first draft. The only problem was that the draft was 1,500 words, and the essay had a 500-word limit. Watching her hack that beautiful draft into a butchered shadow of its former self was awful. Ultimately she gave up and walked away from that story.

Do yourself a favor and learn from Liv: conceive of your story with word budgets in mind, and then aim to write within your limits. In the long run, you'll save yourself time and heartbreak.

Pick a Tense

One useful tool you might want to take advantage of is the variation of the present and past tenses within your essay. Writing in the present tense is a powerful way to grab your reader's attention, as it feels vital and immediate. Writing in the past tense allows you to telescope time, conveying broad events that took place over an extended period. Reflecting on a story in the past tense can also make the reflection feel measured, thoughtful, and mature.

To illustrate the power of the present tense, take a look at the two sentences on the following page:

I'd also like to acknowledge that occasionally a particular theme warrants a bending of the structure rules. To see an example of an essay in which the student writes about more than a single story/experience that changed him, and why it made sense, take a look at Erik's essay about mountain biking in appendix F.

I **was** standing at the open door of an airplane, thousands of feet up in the air, with a parachute on my back, waiting for the thumbs-up to jump.	I **am** standing at the open door of an airplane, thousands of feet up in the air, with a parachute on my back, waiting for the thumbs-up to jump.

Though I only changed one word (**was** to **am**), the shift from past to present brings the moment to life. In this specific case, the present tense is the more effective choice.

Now take a look at the opening of an essay that uses the past tense:

I have always been passionate about business. At five, I launched my business career by reselling items to my triplet brothers (often items that already belonged to them). Eventually, enough capital was raised, and I opened a lemonade stand. Right away, I noticed a trend that when my younger sister was with me, the stand sold more lemonade. To put my theory to the test, we separated. When she sold more cups than I did, I made the executive decision to hire her as a full-time employee, and profits skyrocketed.

In this case, the writer uses the past tense to humorously summarize his youthful escapades that led to his current interest in business. Each of these moments is not important enough to re-experience in the present tense, but they all add up to an amusing overview.

As you structure your essay, know that you might want to use *both* the past and present tenses in different sections of your draft. By writing different parts of your essay in different tenses, you can vary the reader's experience and make it more engaging and dynamic.

To see how one fiercely determined and deliciously funny girl varied her tenses, take a look at Winnie's essay.

Winnie's Common App Essay

OPENING (written in the present tense; pulls the reader into a heightened moment)

I'm standing in the middle of a basketball court, surrounded by 500 teenagers in full Sea Scout uniform. My feet hurt, my palms sweat, and my head pounds. I wait for the next command, hoping it will be an About Face, because that's the only maneuver I can execute without falling over. But instead, I hear "Count off." The kids go down the line counting off: "one, two, one, two, one, two." When it gets to me, I hear my own voice traitorously shout out:

"Three!"

With head hanging low, I make my way

back down the lines of scouts and join the other premature losers on the perimeter of the gym. The average Fleet Drill contains more than 200 commands. I've managed to get out on the third.

BODY: PART ONE (written in the past tense; interrupts the moment to give an overview and background and explains how the writer got to this moment)

Except for this moment, I have always been a super capable Girl Scout. I've sold cookies, camped in the rain, held leadership positions, and earned my Bronze and Silver Awards. But when my Girl Scout troop became a Sea Scout troop, and I was thrust into drill, I met my match.

At this point, a sane person would have given up. "It's not my thing. I'll just watch and cheer for everyone else." But giving up has never been my style, and my troop mates' insistent belief in my ability to improve would not let me off the hook. And so, instead of quitting, I dedicated myself to drill. Every afternoon I dragged my sister into the backyard to call me in flanks, obliques, and to-the-rears. Every night I studied my commands. And every morning I marched around my high school, executing sharp left and right faces to enter hallways, one small, lone scout marching against a sea of smelly teenagers. I didn't do much for my popularity freshman year. What I did do was get better.

BODY: PART TWO (returns to the present tense to finish telling the interrupted story; by writing in the present tense, she heightens the suspense)

A year later, I find myself standing in my second Fleet Drill. If I was filled with fear the first time, I am filled with all-out terror the second. But I am determined. The coxswain starts calling commands, and to my surprise, I execute them perfectly. Other scouts start dropping out, but I keep going. The ranks thin as tens and then hundreds of kids make mistakes and get tapped out. Before I know it, there are only five of us left, surrounded by 495 scouts watching our every move. At this moment, I panic. I can't believe I've gotten this far. I'm sure the others are better. I don't think I can go on. But then I get a hold of myself, push out all the doubting thoughts, focus my mind, and listen. As I do, my body executes the commands. And other kids start making mistakes. Four scouts down to three scouts down to two. Now it's just me and the girl behind me. Then I hear one more call. And suddenly there is no one behind me. The place goes silent. The one thing that seemed utterly impossible has happened. I've won. And I am instantly embraced by every girl in my troop, screaming and whooping, as I cry in their arms.

CLOSING (written in the present tense to make it feel immediate; reflects on the meaning of her story and declares her message)

It would be easy to say that the lessons I learned that day are clichés: work hard, don't give up, allow others to help you, have faith in yourself. But for me, these lessons are not clichés, because they are now stitched into who I am. I walk into my future knowing that how I respond to difficulty and even failure is up to me, and that a future embracing challenge and risk in the context of friendship will lead to the richest life of all.[27]

For more examples of how to vary tenses to different effect, see appendix A. As you structure your story, consider using both the past and present tenses, but be sure to stick to only one tense within each section. The variation might be just the thing to keep your reader alert and intrigued.

One last note: Winnie accomplishes an amazing feat in this essay. She uses understated, slightly wicked, self-deprecating humor in the first half and grows into a more mature, emotionally revealing thoughtfulness in the second half. Hats off to Winnie for sharing her sense of humor and allowing her writing style to mirror her personal evolution.

27　The building blocks of Winnie's essay:
Five Best-Day Words: ambitious, thoughtful, funny, sensitive, intuitive
Story: losing and then winning the Fleet Drill
Message: I embrace challenge and risk in the context of friendship.
Archetypes: Hero, Seeker

CHAPTER 6

IT'S ALL IN THE DETAILS

Once you've got your structure in place, it's time to weave in some of the vibrant qualities that will make your essay shine: voice, the all-important first sentence, quotes, emotion, courage, and a framing device.

Voice

Imagine you go to a movie with a group of people including your cranky grandma, your goofy dad, your cocky older brother, your annoying younger sister, your genius best friend, your clueless neighbor, and your latest crush (I know, worst nightmare, right?), and every single one of you loved it. When you step out of the theater, everyone starts to rave.

Now imagine that I'm there to record this explosion of conversation. I take the recording home, transcribe it, and hand you a script of the conversation without identifying who said what. Think you could assign each line of dialogue to its speaker? I bet you could. Because even when eight people express approval of the very same thing, they all do it differently.

Every person you encounter has his or her own one-of-a-kind vocabulary, grammar, rhythm, humor, edge, and colorful or understated way of expressing him- or herself. In other words, everyone has a distinct voice.

When writing a Common App essay, not only do you want to tell a compelling story that illustrates your message, you also want to avoid sounding like a robot and instead sound like yourself. Fifty kids could all write basketball essays. But if each essay has an original message and is written in the authentic voice of a living, breathing, feeling person, each of those fifty essays will feel fresh, alive, and different. So go for it: while being respectful of the seriousness of your purpose, express and share your unique self in your own voice.[28]

The All-Important First Sentence

When it's finally time to start writing, pay particular attention to your first sentence or two. Use these early words to grab your reader's attention and make them want to read on. Aim to open your essay with energy, conviction, mystery, suspense, wonder, humor, and/or boldness. Remember, your opening line or lines will create your first impression. Here are some of my students' first sentences organized by category (followed by their name in parentheses, because all good writers deserve credit!).

> **A VIVID MOMENT:** There is no better feeling than the excitement and exhilaration of running the ball down the field; it is that fleeting moment of weightlessness, even godliness, when you fly past

---

28 Think about the distinctive voices we've already read: Jackson's confident voice telling the story about building the stairs, Cole's easygoing voice describing his car's flat tire, and Winnie's wry voice taking us through the Sea Scout drills. If you met these kids at a party and spoke to them for a few minutes, you'd be able to figure out who was who, because the voices on the page would match the personalities in the room.

opponents through sheer strength or cunning dexterity. (Aaron)

A CONFESSIONAL STATEMENT: I have a history with perfectionism. (Annie)

A SETUP AND PUNCH LINE: Michael Jordan was put on his school's junior varsity basketball team after his coach told him he was not good enough to make varsity; Oprah Winfrey was fired from her first television reporting job; J.K. Rowling's first draft of *Harry Potter* was sent to the bottom of an editor's trash can; and I received a C on my English midterm. (Erin)

A PHILOSOPHICAL OBSERVATION: The days of August in Manhattan mandate strange juxtapositions of cool, thundering rain and sweltering heat. (Deveron)

A HUMOROUS OBSERVATION: Although sprinting five miles a game, chasing opponents wielding sticks, and getting trampled by 180-pound men might not sound appealing to the average person, I choose to do these things every day . . . and I couldn't be happier. (Matt)

A HUMOROUS CONFESSION: When I lie awake in the middle of the night, I think about shoes. (Isaac)

THE SETTING OF A SCENE: Standing barefoot on

the white sand, surrounded by my extended *ohana*, I mimic the graceful sway of my cousin's hips. (Jillian)

AN UNEXPECTED WORLD: As I walk along the rocky hillside, I hear the elk bugling and the wind whistling through the stillness of the woods. (Alie)

AN UNEXPECTED REALITY: Dear Mom, It's been six years since I last saw you, and so much has happened. (Jessica)

AN UNEXPECTED OBJECT: Weathered, beat up, an octagonal stick with a sand-papery feel. Six feet tall, like me, but with a stiff white scoop and malleable net. Just holding it fills me with adrenaline and joy. (Andrew)

A SURPRISING REVELATION: As I sit in the kitchen working on homework, my mom tries to get me to eat, but I won't. (Meg)

A NERVY DECLARATION: I am going to be the general manager of the New York Yankees. (Peter)

And finally, a category whose scope warrants several examples.

AN INTRIGUING MYSTERY: On the day I was born, I won the lottery. (Isabel)

Polyvinyl chloride: PVC. Infinite in function,

this plastic is manipulated by man to serve his immensely diverse needs. It is the stone, the bronze, the iron of modern man. (Mike)

Frog legs on sticks. Soup with an entire fish in the bowl. Mystery Meat. (Lily)

The Dice Challenge on *Minute to Win It*. The uplift of a jumbo plane. The Coliseum from ancient Rome. And a varsity baseball team that couldn't find its groove. (Jerremy)

Onions, tomatoes, lettuce, celery, cabbage, broccoli, kale, cauliflower, Swiss chard, beets, carrots, turnips, potatoes, peas, beans, summer squash, winter squash, spinach, strawberries, and pumpkins. (Maxwell)

I stand over a man I've just beaten to the ground with a crowbar, his cell phone in my hand. In a rough, gravelly voice, I hit on his girlfriend through the phone while dancing over his body. Without a doubt, this is the best moment of my life. (Dexter)

3.00×10^8 m/s. The speed of light in a vacuum. To me, just one of many values I had to memorize in physics class. That is, until it changed my life forever. (Natalie)

A dynamic opening to your essay will pique your readers' interest and earn their trust and good will. It will lead them into your unique world, captivate them with your individual voice, and make them curious about your experience and point of view.

Quotes

I once had a student write a beautiful essay about photography and how it changed the way she saw the world and lived her life, but she couldn't find an elegant way to begin. I asked if she had a favorite photographer. She did, so I encouraged her to search for a quote from him that expressed the essence of what she loved about taking pictures. After reading dozens of his quotes, she settled on this:

> "A great photograph is a full expression of what one feels about what is being photographed in the deepest sense and is thereby a true expression of what one feels about life in its entirety."
>
> —Ansel Adams

Opening her essay with this quote felt right to her. It established the world of her essay and hinted at the **message** she was building to. Though using a quote in your essay risks being clichéd, if it authentically speaks to your subject or theme, elevates your message, and/or heightens your emotion, feel free to quote away.

An ending quote can also be an effective way to project

your story/message onto a broader stage. I once had a student close his essay by quoting a tweet:

"Maximum expression while I have air in my lungs."

—Kanye West

While most students would hesitate to quote a pop culture figure, in this student's case it made sense. He was applying to extremely innovative and creative business/design/technology programs. In that context, referencing a boundary pusher like Kanye West aligned him with new and unexpected thinking and revealed the breadth of his frame of reference.

As you work on your essay, consider quoting a person you admire (artist, politician, athlete, environmentalist, author, inventor, historical figure, etc.) or a text that inspires (fiction, nonfiction, poem, song lyric, law of physics, recipe, etc.) only if it relates directly or adds a new dimension to your essay. Used judiciously, quotes can be a nice way to reveal what's on your mind.

Emotion

When I told my daughter Sophie that she should write her Common App essay with feeling, she balked. After all, she's a pretty cool cucumber. And though she feels things deeply, she doesn't always let on.

"I don't want my essay to be all hysterical and dramatic," she announced.

"I don't want your essay to be all hysterical and dramatic either," I said.

That's when I explained that to write with real feeling, instead of raising your volume, lower it. Think critically about the story you're telling. Then get quiet and still and state your simple truth. The most powerful way to write with feeling is to quietly state what matters to you and give your reader the knowledge and context to understand why.

How do you do this? How do you honestly access and share your emotional truth? In life, when something big or tragic happens, sometimes the best way to explore it is not to try to explain the whole thing all at once but rather to look for the small, specific, honest moments that reveal or illustrate its impact. To give you an example from my own life, my father passed away a dozen years ago. And in my daily life, I've learned to manage fine without him. But occasionally a moment arises when I feel his loss enormously, like when I'm struggling with something and he's the person who would have known just what to say to help me feel better or figure out what to do. Or when my son, Sam, sits down at the piano and plays a jazz riff like nobody's business, and my eyes instinctively look around the room in search of my father because he would have taken such pleasure in that moment and shared my sense of wonder.

At other times in life, when lots of small, specific moments are unfolding, we aren't even aware that a bigger meaning might be hovering above. But with time, distance, and reflection, the bigger meaning reveals itself. For instance, when I was in high school, my beloved English teacher, Ms. Parker, pulled me aside one day to tell me how moved she was by a personal essay I'd written. It was no big deal, just a two-minute conversation in the middle of a busy day. But when I grew older and wanted to muster the confidence to become a professional writer, that throwaway moment was one of several that bolstered and nourished me.

Another example of small moments adding up to a bigger realization relates to my younger daughter. My third child, Mia, was born into a lively, bookish, music-filled, and soccer-playing whirlwind of a family. By the time she was a toddler, the little pipsqueak had developed a devilish sense of humor, a fabulous sense of style, and a no-holds-barred twinkle in her eye. It wasn't until we'd all started calling her Little Miss Mischief that I realized this shrimp of a genius had somehow managed to carve out her own territory in our boisterous family and make herself not only heard but also adored. It wasn't anything I noticed along the way. But when it all added up, a larger, extremely emotional truth was revealed: no matter where in the world this child lands, she'll be just fine.

I tell these stories to show you can access emotions from the inside out (exploring the small, deeply felt, specific moments that lead you to a big, life-changing experience or realization) or from the outside in (the small, specific moments might not have been deeply felt when you were living each one, but when you reflect on the sum total, a deeply felt, overarching truth becomes clear). Whether the emotion comes in the small moments or in the big realization, your reader will be moved by how dynamically you live your life and reflect on it.

This reminds me of an exercise my class did in my graduate screenwriting program. It was called "Hot Objects." On a given day, we were all asked to bring in a single object that was emotionally loaded. One by one we each described our physical object in extreme detail and then opened up to speak about why the object was emotionally "hot" for us. More than twenty years later, I still remember the objects that were discussed that day: a bracelet received from a former lover; a crocheted blanket made by a recently deceased grandmother; a spider pin given by a cold mother to her longing daughter; a tiny baby shoe held in the hand of a new father. As class members opened up and shared pieces of their inner lives, it became impossible not to care about them. No matter how annoying or arrogant or even boring I might have found them the week before, hearing them speak their emotional truth humanized them and made me want to root for them. That is the power of sharing yourself with others. And that is a power you want to tap into as you tell your story with feeling.

If you'd like to read an essay I find particularly moving, take a look at the following one. Grant is an exceptionally gifted musician and composer. His essay does more than just tell the story of an impressive accomplishment; it also shares his personal context and reveals the emotional connection he feels to his story.

Grant's Common App Essay

One muggy and oppressively hot summer afternoon in the 1950s, my great-uncle Irwin and my grandfather

Leon knocked on the door of an inn in northwestern Massachusetts. Irwin had come from New York City because he wanted to hear Leonard Bernstein conduct Beethoven's Third Symphony at Tanglewood. Leon was only there because he knew how to drive their Ukrainian father's car. The inn door was opened by a plump woman who informed the brothers that there were no available rooms, but they could sleep in the barn if they wanted to. They did. Two generations later, Irwin was the only person in my huge family who understood me, because he and I were the only two musicians of the bunch. So when I found out that I had been accepted into Tanglewood Institute's Composition Program, I chose to spend the day before the program began in New York with Uncle Irwin before saying good-bye and heading north.

My days at Tanglewood were filled with ardent musical study. I sat in on master classes with visiting composers, studied music theory for hours on end, and wrote the most music I have ever been able to get out onto paper. I bonded with my fellow musicians in the program and created friendships that will last forever. On the evening of July 15, I was sitting in the dining hall when I got the call that Uncle Irwin had passed away earlier that evening. I was devastated. It was as if, in such a place of creativity and collaboration, the music stopped. The only family member that I could deeply relate to was gone. It felt finite; the double bar had been etched in black ink.

The following week, when the ideas for final projects were due, I decided that I was going to write a surrealist memorial to my uncle—a requiem of sorts—to commemorate his beginnings in the very place where I was now studying. I named the piece "hot summer night [requiem for a passed new england evening]" and wrote it in about ten days as the music flowed from the ether of my imagination onto the page. It was both the hardest and easiest piece I have ever written. It took the form of three movements, which included electronically sampled crickets, a male choir, a string quartet, percussion, and a barbershop quartet that aimed to create a sonic world that would fulfill the memory of a man who found the greatest joy in music. Although I faced many challenges with the practical production of the piece—scheduling rehearsals, convincing people to show up, even finding rehearsal space in a rainstorm—there was nothing like the sound of the thirty-five musicians performing it at the final concert. It culminated in a feeling of fulfillment like nothing else in the entire world.

Participating in Tanglewood Institute's Composition Program was an amazing opportunity. I learned how to be firm in my intention but flexible in my execution. I was dealing with other musicians my age who had busy schedules in addition to my rehearsals. I figured out how to coordinate and inspire people to give it their all while creating something significant. I practiced humility while treating the piece as a living, breathing creation, which fostered even more collaboration, eventually leading to a successful performance.

Though Uncle Irwin never lived to hear the piece performed, he continues to live on in the music. He began his musical journey at Tanglewood and metaphorically ended it with the closing notes of my piece in the very same place. The piece sings of joy, hope, and fond memory as well as sadness and the resolute finality of death. My summer, and the piece itself, confirmed that music will always be a unifying and grounding force in my life and a way to explore and share my truth with the world.[29]

---

29   The building blocks of Grant's essay:
Five Best-Day Words: outgoing, generous, thoughtful, intelligent, hardworking
Story: attending the Composition Program at Tanglewood Institute
Message: Music is and will be the greatest force in my life.
Archetypes: Leader, Seeker, Artist
Structure:
Opening (158 words): Flashes back more than sixty years to his great-uncle and grandfather at Tanglewood, then gives background information about Grant's musical connection to his great uncle and his own plan to go to Tanglewood.
Body (316 words): Tells the story of his experience at Tanglewood including the **beginning** (studying, learning), **middle** (learning of uncle's death, deciding to write requiem in his memory, rehearsing), and **ending** (triumphant performance).
Closing (174 words): Reflects on this experience, discusses what he learned, and declares his message.
One last note: Grant did a great job sharing how his experience was shaped by someone who died, but he never let the essay become about the person who died.

When someone writes a piece with such an open heart, it's hard to read it and not be moved. And you can bet that the college admissions officers who saw this remembered not only his achievements but also his humanity.

Courage

When I was seventeen and applying to college, I was in the middle of an experience I felt I had to write about. Someone I loved dearly was locked in a brutal battle with anorexia. Watching her slowly starve herself over the last part of my junior year and first part of my senior year was devastating. Early on, I wanted to stop living my life so I could devote myself to helping her get healthy. But over time I realized that no amount of my love and support could make her better. Getting better was something she would have to do for herself. It was a hard lesson to learn, and one that really marked my transition from childhood to adulthood.

Though I no longer have a copy of that essay, I know if I were to read it today it would reveal a girl who didn't run from painful complexity but rather engaged with it, explored it, wrestled with it, and ultimately inched toward a new understanding and even hope. My life in that moment might not have been particularly pretty or even remotely picture-perfect, but it was real and honest and alive and human. I wasn't just living my life. I was actively thinking about how I wanted to live my life.

I share this story with you in case your life has been less than rosy. If your family has struggled or your academic record is imperfect, don't worry that you don't have a good story to tell. In fact, you might have the very best story of all: that of digging deep, overcoming obstacles, developing maturity and resilience, finding meaning, and moving forward. In this day and age when too many college students are the coddled kids of hovering parents, you might be the refreshing and appealing exception of a student who is really ready to make the most of the opportunities and independence that come with college.

To see a raw, sobering, and inspiring example of one such essay, take a look at the following one. It was written by Tess, a gentle, artistic girl who managed to thrive despite enduring difficult circumstances.

Tess's Common App Essay

At the end of a long day at school, I open my front door and am engulfed by darkness and the smell of stale cigarettes. As I move past the clutter of plastic bags and old leftovers, my stomach growls because I didn't have money for lunch. I turn on the kitchen lights. Cockroaches scurry. I open the fridge: nothing. I look at the water bottles: all empty. I open my backpack, revealing a pile of AP French, physics, chemistry, pre-calc, AP English, AP US history, German IV, and Latin. Tears start to well up.

My father is an alcoholic. When I was in seventh grade, my parents split up. For a while, my mom lived with a new boyfriend, but when I was in eleventh grade they broke up. She couldn't find a new apartment right away, so she and I had to move back into my dad's house. From December 2012 until August 2013, I lived with my two parents under the same roof, but they wouldn't speak to each other. My mom stayed in her makeshift room. She and I only knew how to argue. My dad stayed in the living room, watching sports games, yelling at referees. The worst was seeing him drink and watch pornography. I mostly stuck to my own room, struggling to do homework. I would start it but give up after a couple assignments and instead watch movies, videos, and even read until 4 a.m. I searched for anything that would help me escape to another world.

Toward the end of summer, my mom had saved enough money, and she and I finally moved out of my dad's house into our own apartment. It marked the beginning of my healing process. Our new home was clean, bright, and calm. The fridge was always full. My mom convinced me to go to therapy, both with her and on my own. She learned to open up to me about her past and herself. I learned to change the negative to positive. Miraculously, we found our way back to each other.

My eleventh grade was filled with parties

and people who drank to forget. I cared too much about what others thought. But during the summer, I spent a lot of time by myself. I reconnected with two old friends who are funny and affectionate and care deeply about me. By the end of summer, I was feeling more comfortable with who I am: my body, my sexual orientation, and my own opinions, all things I had struggled with before.

Looking ahead to twelfth grade, I saw an opportunity to start over. I committed myself to eating well, getting enough sleep, and finishing all my homework. I promised myself that I would fulfill my own potential. I am happy to say I have kept that promise. And many of my teachers have noticed the change in me, responding with encouragement and a newfound trust that inspires me to even greater heights.

Eleventh grade was a sad and painful time for me. In twelfth grade, I transformed myself. My days are now filled with hope, hard work, and a passionate sense of purpose. With each new success, it becomes easier for me to be proud of the things I do and proud of who I am.

Last year, when I thought about going to college, I only wanted to get away from the struggles I had at home and at school. This year, I have different reasons to want to go. Now, I am excited to challenge myself, study chemistry and systems engineering, find a nice group of friends I can count on, create strong bonds with my professors, and learn to be truly independent. At last I feel ready to own my own life and determine for myself all that it will be.[30]

Tess's essay works because it lays out her specific struggles and illustrates how she responded to and overcame them. She reveals how she worked to heal her relationship with her mother, made different choices to align herself with more supportive friends, and dedicated herself to succeeding in school, ultimately earning her teachers' respect. And the happy ending to this particular story? Tess's honesty and heart and seriousness of purpose earned her a place at a very prestigious small liberal arts college in the Midwest where she is achieving and contributing in all the ways the admissions committee knew she could and would.

---

30 The building blocks of Tess's essay:
Five Best-Day Words: artistic, dedicated, open, sensitive, curious
Story: overcoming family struggles and investing in herself
Message: By owning my choices and responsibilities, I can create a meaningful life filled with hope and purpose.
Archetypes: Hero, Seeker, Artist

Framing Device

As you structure your draft, one tool you might consider is a framing device, which is a vibrant or personal story that you use to open and close your essay. Recently, I worked with a student named Ava who'd crafted an intellectual vitality essay on what she'd learned from writing a paper about a Supreme Court decision. While researching the case, she discovered that most people have fierce political opinions, but few are willing to really listen to and try to understand their opponents. By researching both sides of this case, she discovered that people generally hold their beliefs after thoughtful consideration, and if she wants to learn and grow, she must be willing to open her mind to differing opinions.

Ava wrote a strong essay about her research and discovery, but she was looking for a way to give the draft more feeling. "If I can make it more personal and emotional, I think it will have more impact." So I asked one of my favorite questions: how did the lessons you learned from writing the paper change your life? After thinking for a moment, she confessed, "Actually, they changed my relationship with my sister."

Ava and her sister had been in conflict. After writing the paper, when she finally stopped to imagine their troubles from her point of view, she was suddenly filled with both compassion and forgiveness. She'd found her framing device.

So Ava wrote a brief opening about her conflict with her sister and explained how she used her research paper as a distraction from their problems. She then closed her essay with a brief description of what happened when she applied the lessons learned from the paper to her relationship with her sister, and how they offered Ava a path back to her. The intellectual vitality essay was now framed by a one-of-a-kind, authentic, moving story with very real emotional stakes. Do you see how this elevates the entire reading experience without changing a single word in the essay's body? And it shows how she carries over what she learns in school to how she lives her life. Now that's a great framing device!

To see an example of another effective framing device, please read Chloe's essay. She tells the story of transitioning from gymnastics to cheer, but she frames her story with an unrelated but heightened emotional moment.

Chloe's Common App Essay

I am standing on top of a thirty-foot cliff watching the sun shine on the water below. I look down, wanting to jump into the waves, wanting to be free, but I hesitate. My mind races, my heart pounds. And I wonder: Do I have the courage? And does my story include such enormous leaps of faith?

Eleven years ago, when I was six, my father died of cancer. I was thrown into a state of grief and shock. I turned inward and became extremely shy and quiet. My ability to learn was hindered, and I almost had to repeat first grade. What saved me and acted as my therapy was gymnastics. Gymnastics was grounding. Within one week of starting, I jumped three reading levels and began to focus in school. I grew passionate about the sport and wanted to devote all my time to it. The longer I did it, the more I committed to it, the more serious I became. I ended up devoting ten years to it, traveling the nation for competitions and practicing every day for five hours. I learned discipline, dedication, and focus. Gymnastics was my identity.

But after eight years, my love of gymnastics began to fade. The sport that had changed my life was becoming more of a burden than a passion. Rather than acting as a therapy, it was only adding stress and pressure to my life. Even though I knew that my feelings for gymnastics had changed, I couldn't imagine living without it. I was unsure who I would be and was terrified I would regret it if I quit.

Sometimes it takes courage to stop doing something familiar and open yourself up to new possibilities. With time, I realized that change is scary, but life is about taking chances and not worrying about regrets. After almost two years of doing gymnastics with no love for the sport, I finally decided to try something new: cheerleading.

When I walked into my first day of cheer, I felt many mixed emotions. I was unbelievably excited to try something new, but at the same time I was scared. Would I be able to do the new stunts and skills? And more importantly, would I be able to open up and be as outgoing as a cheerleader has to be? All my life I had been shy and reserved. Could I learn to be loud and outgoing, enthusiastic, joyous, and physically expressive? At that first practice, to my own surprise, I discovered I could. I found cheerleading to be great fun and a huge release, and the more I tried on an enthusiastic attitude, the more my own persona changed.

Through cheer, I eventually learned that I had all of the qualities of a cheerleader in me all along. I had just never let them out. Rather than being so reserved, I was now allowing myself to open up and let out all parts of my personality. I became less insecure and accepted myself. And nine months later, at the end-of-season cheer banquet, my transformation was confirmed. My coach stepped to the microphone to announce the team's most important award: Most Improved All-Squad. "For the girl who joined our team as a quiet little gymnast and became a bad-*** cheerleader . . . Chloe!"

So as I stand here on top of the cliff, looking down at the beautiful sea below, I wonder if I can jump. And I finally realize that life is what I choose to make it. With so much behind me and so much ahead, I now understand all of the possibilities of who I can be, what I can do, and what my life can become. I have learned that a life lived openly and outwardly—when you choose to share yourself with others rather than hold yourself inside—is a life lived to its fullest. And so I leap.[31]

When Chloe and I worked together, she knew she wanted to tell the story of transitioning from gymnastics to cheer, but she wanted to find an emotional way to open her story and later declare her message. As we brainstormed and I asked her dozens of questions, I finally got to, "What is the most joyous moment in high school that you can remember?" Right away she thought of a moment while on vacation with her mom, stepdad, and stepsister, standing on top of the cliff and digging deep for the nerve to leap. When I suggested she use that for her framing device, she worried that it was unrelated to the story she was telling. But as soon as I pointed out that it was the perfect metaphor for the lessons she'd learned, she loved the idea.

---

31   The building blocks of Chloe's essay:
Five Best-Day Words: kind, gentle, lively, brave, joyful
Story: quitting gymnastics and starting cheer
Message: To live life to its fullest, I must live openly and outwardly.
Archetypes: Seeker, Dreamer, Hero
Note that Chloe writes her opening and closing paragraphs in the present tense and her body in the past tense. By writing her opening in the present tense she pulls her reader into her story, but then she interrupts the moment and leaves a question unanswered. The body is written chronologically in the past tense. Her closing returns to the present moment and finally answers the unanswered question.

If you imagine your essay as a gift to your reader, your framing device is the paper you wrap it in. Ava wrapped hers in a moving opening and closing about her dad. Chloe wrapped hers in a metaphorical leap of faith. You can find yours by asking how your main story changed the way you think, feel, or live.

Making the Most of This Wonderful Opportunity

Occasionally, I'm asked if there is anything a student should not write about. Except for the obvious—beliefs that are prejudiced, racist, sexist, misogynistic, xenophobic, homophobic, etc., which would make you a profoundly unappealing community member—I like to think most topics are on the table. But remember, no matter what story you choose to share, you'll want to use it to highlight your best qualities, deepest thoughts, and most impactful actions. Always be socially sensitive and empathetic. And if you feel you must share a story about specific struggles with mental illness, it might be best to do so only if you have managed to get on top of your struggles.[32]

There is one last thing to consider. If your transcript is completely covered with your participation in a single activity (i.e., high school volleyball, club volleyball, summer volleyball), consider writing about something other than that activity. The colleges will already see that you are hugely dedicated to that pursuit, so you don't have to tell

---

32 For one such example, take a look at the Female Hero's Common App essay in appendix A, in which she shares a story about struggling with and overcoming anorexia.

them that. Instead use your essay to round out their picture of you, share something more personal, show your creative side, surprise them with another unexpected talent/sensitivity/ experience, or reveal your unique brand of intellectual vitality. Of course, if the most important story you have to tell is your volleyball story, you may. Just make sure you use it to tell them something they don't already know . . . and something that no other applicant could say. After all, that's how you'll make the most of this wonderful opportunity.

*****

Remember that list of words I had you read out loud at the beginning of this book? I'd like to ask you to read them aloud one more time:

message	generosity
character	ambition
passion	work ethic
purpose	authenticity
embracing of diversity	emotion
bridge-building	leadership qualities
curiosity	suspense
intellectual vitality	conflict
adaptability	vivid descriptions
resilience	sincerity
willingness to change	enthusiasm
willingness to take chances	intentionality
achievement	struggle

growth	originality
confidence	honesty
new understanding	humor
initiative	accomplishments
impact	goals
one colorful, lively story	appreciation of nature
beginning, middle, ending	appreciation of culture
motivation	pattern of service
drive	maturity
making choices	sensitivity
taking actions	voice
innovation	open-mindedness
creativity	unique quality

By now, you understand what this is: a list of the qualities to explore, share, illustrate, and include in your essay. Use this list as your North Star. No matter how far and wide you travel, nor how dark the essay-writing night might get, these words will always guide you home.

It's official. I've now shared everything you need to know to write a unique, meaningful, moving Common App essay. If knowledge is power, then you are all-mighty. So it's time for my promised brief, practical step-by-step guide to writing your Common App essay. If you diligently follow through on every step, you will finish with an essay that is a clear expression of who you are and what special value you will bring to a college community.

Though it might seem unnecessary, I'm going to ask you to write or type your answers through all the steps. I believe you will find it helpful later to be able to go back and read through your notes (not to mention when you're looking for an idea for a supplemental essay!). So turn the page.

CHAPTER 7

A STEP-BY-STEP GUIDE TO WRITING YOUR COMMON APP ESSAY

Read the Common App essay prompts: Start by reading the Common App prompts. If they immediately spark an idea of what to write about, make notes. If not, don't worry. You'll discover plenty of ideas as we move through this guide.

Why college? Make a list of the reasons you want to go to college. Articulating your purpose will focus you throughout this challenging task.

Academics: Make a list of your favorite academic subjects and why you like each one. Convey your genuine love of learning and intellectual curiosity.

Extracurriculars: Make a list of your top five extracurricular activities and why you like each one. Describe your dedication to the choices you make. Reflect on how they have challenged you, what you have learned from each one, and how those lessons carry over to other parts of your life.

Five Best-Day Words: Make a list of the five words that best describe you on your best day. Whatever essay you end up writing should convey these important qualities.

Five Worst-Day Words: Make a list of the five words that best describe you on your worst day. Do they remind you of specific moments in your high school life when you were struggling through a significant conflict/transition? Might that conflict/transition be something worth writing about?

Archetype: Make a list of the one, two, or three archetypes that sound most like you. To review their definitions, refer to page 32. Remember, there is no right or wrong or better or worse, and we are all made up of many archetypes. Your goal in choosing your archetype or archetypes is simply to allow their definitions to guide you to your message.

Begin to search for your story by using story prompts: Make a list of the most heightened moments (challenging, rewarding, scary, joyous) you can remember from your high school years. (These moments do not necessarily have to be related to school; they might be with immediate family, extended family, and friends, while traveling, in extracurriculars, etc.) Ask yourself what accomplishments you are most proud of. Think about the times you made a real difference. Brainstorm possible stories by asking yourself all the questions on the list of story prompts on pages 53-56.

Look for a big impact: Make a list of any texts, theories, or historical events you've encountered that have had an impact on you. Make a list of your favorite resources: books, poems, lyrics, newscasts, blogs, podcasts, films, YouTube channels, etc. Make a list of the people you admire: scientists, journalists, artists, inventors, athletes, fictional characters, etc. Consider the ways they inspire you and change the way you live your life (think of Molly and how *Walden* inspired her to quit her club swim team).

Unique point of view: Make a list of any sensitivities, ideas, or themes that fascinate you and drive your choices and actions (think of Josh's dedication to doing good in the world).

Accentuate the positive: If your most compelling quality is not your academic record, figure out what is and find a story to illustrate it (just as Cole—who worked in the pizza parlor—illustrated his positive attitude).

Intellectual vitality: Are you someone who is energized by new ideas? If so, look for an experience that shows you coming alive inside or outside a classroom. What actions do you take when your mind and imagination are captivated by a new idea, concept, or formula? (In Nathan's case, he wrote about how his Parisian grandfather launched him on a lifetime of curiosity and reading.)

Learning differences: If you feel the most important story you have to tell is the way you have overcome a learning difference (like Brian, who wrote about dyslexia), spend no more than one-third of the essay on your struggles and at least two-thirds on how you have overcome them. If you have learning differences but don't feel they are your most important story to tell, feel free to share an experience that shows who you are outside of your learning differences (like Siena, who wrote about interning in Berlin).

Creativity: If creativity is what drives you, describe a project that challenged you, inspired you, stretched you outside your comfort zone, presented obstacles and demanded innovation, and helped you discover beauty, truth, a new perspective, or something unexpected about yourself or your life (just as Annie's video project helped her discover that she is comfortable with the unknown).

Think outside the box: Want to write about an unusual or unexpected passion (like Samuel's love for fantasy football)? Go ahead, but do it with discipline. Be specific. Spell out all the ways it challenges you and reveal all the qualities it fosters that will make you a great college student: work ethic, innovative thinking, creativity, community building, etc.

Message: What do your word lists, archetypes, experiences, influences, and ideas say about you? Make a list of possible messages that begin to emerge (the things that give your life meaning, get you up in the morning, keep you up at night, make you feel most alive and hopeful/energized for the future). Usually as you bounce among your word lists, archetypes, experiences, and possible messages, a favorite experience or archetype will rise to the surface. If you have a favorite experience, how does it illustrate your archetype? If you have a favorite archetype, look for an experience that shows you in its light.

As you reflect on your **experience/story** and **archetype**, focus on how you struggled and try to tease out how the experience changed you, what it meant to you, or what you learned from it. Get quiet and still and state your simple truth, the **message** you want your reader to know about you. To find it, explore the tiny, specific moments that add up to the bigger, emotional insight that hovers above.

Outline: When you find the struggle-filled story that best illustrates your unique, passionate, purposeful character and you can articulate the message you'll declare at the end of your essay, create your essay's **outline**. Think about how best to tell your story and thoughtfully **structure** your essay. Remember: sometimes it's powerful to start in the middle of a heightened moment and then go back to fill in the background. Other times it's most effective to give a brief history and then tell your whole story in the present tense as if it's unfolding in the moment. Alternatively, you could simply tell the whole story in the past tense as it happened. In any case, decide if you will write each section in the present or past tense. Remember, there are many ways to effectively structure your essay. Experiment a bit. Maybe even play with time. (For examples of different structures, look at the opening, body, and closing of some of the essays in appendix A.)

Make sure to include your chronological story's **beginning** (problem), **middle** (struggle and growth), and **ending** (resolution). Finally, decide what will be included in the **opening, body,** and **closing** and give yourself a **word budget** for each section (50–200/350–500/50–300 is a good place to start; if you like firmer boundaries, try starting with 100/400/150).

Consider using a **framing device** to open and close your

essay to make it more personal, emotional, or vibrant (think of Ava's evolving relationship with her sister and Chloe's leap of faith).

First draft: Once you have an outline and word budgets for each section, you're ready to begin writing. As you work on the first draft, remember to look for opportunities to subtly tease out some of the qualities colleges look for: intellectual vitality, adaptability and resilience, open-mindedness, work ethic, generosity toward others in your community, the ways in which you inspired others to fulfill their potential, a pattern or history of service to others, curiosity, embracing of diversity and difference, bridge-building, and, of course, character, passion, and purpose.

Remember also to include the obstacles you encountered, mistakes you made, failures you suffered, how you overcame them, why the stakes were so high, and the ways you exemplified resilience and bounced back. Show how you changed over time with experience. Illustrate how you evolved and grew. (Note: when discussing struggle, spend fewer words on your bad times and more on how you turned things around.)

In your closing, examine what happened and evaluate it with **critical thinking**. Be sure to declare your **message** loud and clear. This is where your reader should be moved by your passion and dedication. (For examples of this, take a look at the closings of several of the sample essays included in this book.)

Rewrite: A first draft is just that—a *first* draft. Now it's time to make it better.

Make sure the story has a **beginning**, **middle**, and **ending**.

Double check that it also has **conflict**, **obstacles**, **struggle**, and **resolution**.

Is there an opportunity to use some **dialogue**? If so, it can be a great way to stay in the present, active, specific voice.

Are you telling (flatly narrating/overexplaining/commenting from the outside) or showing (dramatically taking your reader into specific moments with careful, precise observations/images/scenes/dialogue)? Remember, in your opening and body you want to dynamically show. Only in your closing, while declaring your message, do you want to tell.

Go through and heighten the **imagery**, **suspense**, and **humor**. (Life can be crazy, so let your funny out!)

Have you written in your own **authentic, conversational voice** (your goal), or are you trying to sound like someone you think an admissions person wants you to sound like and thereby wasting your one opportunity to make yourself genuinely known?

Have you told the story with **feeling**? To move your reader and make a strong impression, you must be willing to write with emotion. So get quiet and still and state what you've learned/discovered about yourself—your truth. State it simply, openly, and with pride.

If you've chosen to use both the **present and past tenses**, make sure you are consistent within each section.

Check your **first sentence**. Does it grab the reader's attention? Is it a vivid moment, confessional statement, setup and punch line, humorous or unexpected observation, revelation, declaration, or intriguing mystery? For examples, please refer back to pages 108–111. But don't be limited by these suggestions. They are only intended to spur your imagination!

Would the use of a **quote** elevate your essay, or is it unnecessary?

Listen to your sentences out loud as if you are listening to a piece of music. Make sure you've got **variety** in the language and length and style of your sentences so the rhythm of your essay is pleasing to the ear and ever changing.

When you get to your closing, is there an opportunity to **circle back** to something from your opening?

Polish: Check to see if your writing is **clear** and **straightforward**. Read your draft out loud; it will help you hear your mistakes. Could a stranger read your essay and easily follow it?

Ideally, the exercise of writing this essay has helped you figure out something important about yourself (your **message**). Make sure it is clearly articulated at the end of your essay.

Trim, trim, trim. Eliminate repetition and rambling. Work hard to say more with less. Respect your reader by being concise. And if—after you've said everything you need to say—your final draft is less than 650 words? That's fine: 650 words isn't the goal; it's the limit.

If you find your draft is running extremely long, look for pieces of your story to eliminate or search for ways to give a briefer, more sweeping description of a less imperative part of the experience.[33]

Get feedback: After you finish each draft, find a couple of trusted readers to give you honest, constructive feedback. Ask your readers these questions:

* Is my story clearly told?

* Does my writer's voice sound like me?

* What personal qualities does my essay illustrate?

* What particular value will I bring to a college campus?

* What do you think is my message?

---

33 Remember composer Grant's essay about the Tanglewood Institute? His outline included the following notes:

At first rehearsal for vocalists, only two out of twenty-five showed up.
I panicked.
How to get overcommitted singers to memorize unaccompanied choral music in ten days?
That night, called meeting of chorus.
Explained that piece was dedicated to uncle who passed away.
"Don't do just because cool performance art. Do this for me as a friend."
Next rehearsal everyone showed up.

As soon as he started writing his essay, he realized he did not have room for all the detail in this particular moment, so he ultimately wrote a briefer, more sweeping description to convey the same ideas:

Although I faced many challenges with the practical production of the piece—scheduling rehearsals, convincing people to show up, even finding rehearsal space in a rainstorm . . .

Though it's hard to cut content, and specifics are always good, necessity will sometimes require you to surrender some details to make room for your most important actions and all-important message.

* Were you moved by my essay? In what way?
* Do you see any errors in punctuation, spelling, grammar, verb tense, logic?

Try to take in your readers' constructive comments with an open mind, but don't allow yourself to be too swayed by any one person. Remember, if you ask ten people how to tell your story, they will suggest ten different ways. Have confidence in the thoughtful, informed, and strategic way you've done this work. But if all your readers are having the same issues, you should definitely address their concerns.[34]

Before you click *Submit*: Continue to rewrite and refine until everyone who reads your essay can answer all of the previous questions. Then proofread your essay, and have at least two more people proofread it for you too. Remember to check your grammar and punctuation.

Never exceed the word limit. I repeat: NEVER EXCEED THE WORD LIMIT. I've heard that students who exceed the word limit are put in a pile of *People Who Do Not Follow Instructions.* You do not want to end up in that pile.

Click *Submit*: Be proud of the journey you've taken. Though it's been hard work, it is a once-in-a-lifetime adventure leading you to a pure expression of who you are in this pivotal moment in your life.

---

34 If you'd like to see the rewriting process in action, please take a look at appendix G. In it, you will see my tech-savvy student Cece's original draft, the new outline we created together, an intermediate draft along with my notes to her, and her final draft. I hope it will inspire you to keep at it until your essay sings.

CHAPTER 8

THOSE DARNED SUPPLEMENTALS

Though this book is about writing the Common App essay, please understand that everything I've told you about writing this personal statement holds true for your supplemental essays too. Each one—no matter its length—should be thoughtfully brainstormed and outlined. Each one should have an archetype and articulated message. Each one should be authentic and moving. Each one demands and should receive your full attention. After all, if you're applying to a school because you might want to go there, why would you give it anything less than everything you've got?

As for the very common "Why do you want to go here?" supplemental essay question, here's what you should keep in mind. When the colleges read these essays, they're looking for a combination of thoughtfulness (Have you done your homework and confirmed that their school can actually meet your needs?) and enthusiasm (If colleges offer you one of the coveted spots in their freshman class, they want to think you might actually come!). So do some research and be sure to include in your essay all the ways they will meet your academic needs (possible majors and minors, a couple classes that sound exciting, a professor you would like to learn from, a specific study abroad program or destination, a research opportunity, a field experience, an internship opportunity, interdepartmental opportunities). If the question is framed broadly, also include the ways they will meet your personal needs (a community service opportunity, particular clubs or intramural sports teams you'd like to join, performing arts opportunities, religious organizations on campus, etc.). In both cases, make sure you use correct names. (If they call their study abroad program Experiences Abroad, do not refer to it as Study Abroad!) If you have enough words, refer to your campus visit (did you visit a department? meet a professor? audit a class?) or the tour/information session or interview you attended. Establish how your track record (the things you've done in high school) sets you up to make the most of what they offer at the college. Explore the synergy between you and the school and craft a strong connection between the two. And do all this with thoughtfulness, sincerity, and genuine passion. After all, just like when you're "prom-posing" to the girl or guy of your dreams, the college you are courting might need a little convincing. So don't be shy—declare your affection in your own unique voice!

Finally, understand that your Common App essay shares who you are so that a college can decide if you are a good fit for them. This essay allows you to illustrate all the specific ways they are a good fit for you too.

EPILOGUE

An update on my daughter Sophie: at the end of her college application process, she received acceptances from many wonderful schools and decided to attend Haverford College in Pennsylvania. She wanted small, she wanted liberal arts, she wanted a city nearby, and she wanted snow. Just as important, they wanted her.

It's been said that getting into college isn't a competition to be won but a match to be made. I'm confident that Sophie made the right match. How do I know? Well, she finally let me read her essay. In it I discovered that my daughter, my firstborn, is a Seeker who is happiest when she is engaging in big challenges as part of a close-knit team—and then writing a funny sonnet about it afterward. At Haverford, the team is small enough for her to play an important role. They value their honor code, and so does she. And snow is pretty much guaranteed.

As a parent, it will be hard to let her go. But she's ready. You can hear that in her essay too.

After Sophie finally shared her essay with me, she asked, "What about you, Mom? What's your archetype? What would be your message?"

I had to think about that. And what I came up with is this: I'm an Adventurer who is happiest at the top of a mountain I've never stood on or in the center of a new city without a cell phone but with a map. I'm also a Caregiver who is just as happy helping my kids off to school. The first kid is launched. I have two more to go. Then, I hope, my husband will invite me to the airport and hand me an envelope.

I can't wait to discover where it takes me.

Bon voyage.

TWO SAMPLE ESSAYS OF EACH ARCHETYPE

Following you will find two sample essays of each archetype, one written by a female student and one written by a male student.[35] I tried to include plenty of variety in terms of stories (about internships, sports, travel, extracurricular activities, jobs, family, arts, etc.), messages, and structures. Don't feel you have to read all of these sample essays; just have a look at the ones that seem relevant to you.

Though I have put each of these essays into a single archetype, in truth most essays and most students will fall into two or three. That's okay. We are not using these archetype categories to limit our thinking but rather to help us brainstorm possible messages and find the stories that best illustrate those messages (as well as the unique quality we will bring to a college campus).

Please take special note of the students who bravely write about the very real challenges in their lives and how they have responded to them. Also note that every single story has an element of **struggle** that leads to **growth/change** and **understanding**. Yours should too!

---

35 Of course, when my daughter Sophie read a draft of this book, she immediately objected to the binary-ness of one female and one male sample. "Why do you even have to say if it's written by a girl or boy? Why does it matter?" When I countered that it was extremely important to me to show that young women can be Heroes and Leaders and young men can be Dreamers and Caregivers, she relented. Let's hope by the time Sophie's kids are applying to college, such categorizations will no longer be needed.

Finally, know that every one of the essays in this book came from a real, live teenager with strengths and weaknesses just like yours. These students went through the college admissions process and got into schools including Harvard, MIT, UC Berkeley, USC, Wellesley, Michigan, Kenyon, BU, and wonderful regional colleges you've probably never heard of. I'm happy to report that every one of them landed at a school that deeply valued what they had to offer, which means they ended up exactly where they belonged. Despite whatever apprehension you might feel now, I promise that if you do this work thoughtfully, you will, too. And, just so you know, research now shows that where you go to college matters a whole lot less than what you do once you get there. So wherever you land, make the most of it!

THE HERO: **a resilient, ambitious crusader who takes courageous, difficult action to improve the world and prove his/her worth.**

Example 1: I am calling Meg a Hero because her life-and-death struggle leads her to want to help others.

Female Hero

As I sit in the kitchen working on homework, my mom tries to get me to eat, but I won't. After weeks of skipping meals, I am deteriorating into a walking skeleton. Like every week, I ask to go to tumbling class. Like every week, my parents say no. As I cry and scream, I realize that I can't live like this anymore. I can't conquer my anxiety alone. My parents ask what I need, and I confess, "I don't know. I just know I need more help than you can give me and more help than I can give myself."

The summer before ninth grade, everything had been going fine. But when I started at a brand new high school, I became anxious. Before I knew it, I was no longer in control of myself. I came to focus my anxiety on my body, starved myself, and overexercised. Eventually, I was admitted to UCLA Medical Center. Diagnosed with anorexia nervosa, I was nearly dead.

When I first got to UCLA, I was scared and lonely and didn't care if I lived or died. I went to therapy three times each day and moved numbly through my recurring schedule. With each passing day, nothing got easier for me. But then I met my occupational therapist, Leah. With her help, I began to turn a corner.

Leah shared with me the skills I needed to change my outlook and have the strength I had always strived for. She taught me to see past my mind's misconceptions about my body and see the truth and beauty about myself, inside and out. She encouraged me stop pushing away bad thoughts but to confront them and everything inside of me. She even sat with me in art class one day while I finished ten different projects I had abandoned because I thought they were not good enough. "Imperfection is perfection."

Three months later, I checked out of UCLA but continued to go back for another three months of daily outpatient treatment. Three years later, I still keep in touch with Leah. I have gone to visit girls currently in the program so they can see the beauty of recovery. The first time I visited, there was a group of five girls, all eleven years old, all devastatingly sick. At that moment, I knew I wanted to spend my life helping kids who are dealing with this unbelievably difficult illness.

For the rest of high school, I continued to dedicate myself to my therapy, my schoolwork, and my friends. I spent the past two summers in

Boston and Chicago, taking abnormal psychology and developmental children's psychology classes. I loved meeting new kids, exploring the cities, and dedicating myself to the rigorous academics, and I am so proud of all the hard work I put in.

Today, I am able to take care of myself and get through all that is thrown at me. Despite the bumps in the road, perhaps because of them, I know now I will always stand tall and be proud of all that I am.

When I think about where I will be in a year, I feel nervous. For so long, I have dreamed of going to college, studying psychology, and striving to be all I can be. I am a girl who suffered through anorexia, but anorexia does not define me. What defines me is my desire to live. When I was young, I lost my sense of hope. I spent years fighting hard to get it back. Now, I am so grateful to be able to embrace life and see the true beauty in every moment. I want to dedicate my life to children who are going through the same struggles I went through. Helping them rediscover hope will fill my life with the greatest meaning and purpose I can possibly imagine.

Example 2: I am calling Max a Hero because he takes brave action to improve his school and inform his peers.

Male Hero

Spring break, 2009. My dad offers to take me on a trip. He picks the city, Washington, D.C., and asks me what I want to see. I think I'll like the Spy Museum or the space capsules at the Air and Space Museum. But what I end up loving the most is the empty, silent chamber of the House of Representatives. It fills me with a sense of power and possibility. This is where change begins.

At the start of my junior year in high school, I was discouraged to notice that my peers were not engaged in what was going on around the country and the world. So I set myself a goal to change that and founded and became president of my school's chapter of the National Speech and Debate Association.

By December, I wanted to reach an even larger audience. So I got in touch with the presidents of our Young Democrat and Republican Clubs and offered to organize a formal debate between them. They enthusiastically accepted.

In the lead-up to the event, I wrote the discussion topics and determined the structure for the debate. I asked each of the clubs to create a five-person panel, research the questions, and prepare. Though I didn't expect much, I was stunned four days before the debate when I arrived at school and saw the clubs independently had put up dozens of posters.

On the day of the debate, I anticipated an audience of fifty. So when 350 of my peers and teachers showed up, I was terrified. "What will I say?" I wondered. "Will I stutter?" Then I quickly composed myself and rang the bell to begin.

The first few questions about gun control and government-funded community college went very well. Both teams were extremely informed, and their responses enlightened the crowd and me. As we neared the end, I wanted to create a more spontaneous interaction, so I improvised the last question.

"Do you think the U.S. should accept Syrian refugees?"

The Democrats' panelist was the first to speak. He responded yes and explained why.

Then the Republican panelist—who happened to be one of my close friends—answered.

"No, we should not allow them into this country because a large percentage of Muslim Syrians are terrorists."

When I heard this comment, I was shocked. The whole room fell silent and all eyes turned to me, the moderator. Though I desperately didn't want to have to call out my friend in front of everyone, I knew I could not let this racist comment stand. So I asked one follow-up question.

"Do you believe that a religion is defined by its extremists?"

Before my friend had time to respond, the president of the Democrat Club asked another question.

"Does the KKK represent all Christians?"

My friend froze. After what felt like an hour, she quietly and simply responded.

"No."

In that moment, she recognized her bias was indefensible. And I felt grateful that the record had been set straight.

After the debate, dozens of kids thanked me for organizing it and offered to help with the next one. I felt proud that I had fought to inform the students, encourage them to look beyond their individual lives, and accomplish my initial goal.

When I was a boy in D.C., I sensed the power and possibility of those working to improve my country. Now, as a high school senior, I know the challenge and satisfaction of working to improve my school. Soon, as a college student studying politics and government, I will be glad to engage with a broader, more diverse peer group.

I don't know if my future will take me back to that chamber that captivated me when I was a boy, but I do know I want my life to be guided by the search for unbiased truth and the will to stand against injustice.

THE SEEKER: an inquirer and thinker who seeks truth and understanding through information and knowledge; pursues wisdom, confidence, and mastery; and promotes continuous learning.

Example 1: I am calling Kira a Seeker because her passionate pursuit of knowledge defines who she is and the work she wants to do.

Female Seeker

Two feet, two hands, and a head found buried in separate bags scattered throughout Bronson Canyon in 2012. Two years later, a large piece of skin was discovered in the Bronson Canyon Bat Cave. Who was the victim and who was the murderer? What was the motivation? Why Bronson Canyon? These were the questions forensic scientists addressed in the Hollywood Dismemberment Case.

I have always been fascinated by mysteries. I have an unyielding desire to discover how and why things work together and what makes people tick. Compelled by Agatha Christie novels and biology lectures at school, I have uncovered my passion for learning about hidden connections and meanings that cannot be understood simply with the naked eye. This is why I intend to attend medical school to become a forensic pathologist.

During the summer before my junior year, I had the opportunity to attend the National Student Leadership Conference for Neuroscience and Psychology. The conference was ten days long at American University in Washington, D.C. We listened to lectures, did labs including a sheep brain and cow eye dissection, and attended workshops that developed our leadership skills. Through this conference, I learned that I love research and am willing to take risks to pursue knowledge. I did not know anyone at the conference and expected to have a difficult time making friends. At school, people say it's weird that I love dissections, am constantly trying to learn more, and enjoy other stereotypically nerdy activities such as reading comic books. At this conference, my peers accepted my passions and actually explored them with me. I have never felt more comfortable and overjoyed with a group of people in my life.

Last spring, in chasing my passion for mysteries and scientific investigation, I emailed the LA Department of Medical Examiner-Coroner in search of a summer internship. Because one must be eighteen years or older to work inside the autopsy room, I learned I was not eligible and expected this to be the end of my journey until I turned eighteen. So when I received an email from the department inviting me to their West Coast Training Conference directed at professionals, I jumped at the chance.

To attend the conference, I missed three days of school, but it was a worthwhile and incredible opportunity. The nine hours each day were filled with lectures from professionals about the physics of explosions, the handling of high-profile cases, blood spatter analysis, the legal distinctions made in homicide cases, psychoactive botanicals, and so much more. I was surrounded by professionals, which was both intimidating and exciting. Many people asked my age and were surprised to hear my answer. I became friends with homicide detectives Sean Irving and Oscar Valenzuela, who, at the end of the conference, told me that they wanted to keep in touch to see where I ended up because I had inspired them and given them hope for my generation.

So, what pieces of information finally connected to solve the Hollywood Dismemberment Case? The feet, hands, head, and piece of skin all belonged to one victim named Hervey Medellin. The murderer, Campos Martinez, was the heartbroken lover of the victim and a Hollywood chef. Medellin was allegedly going to break up with Martinez, providing a motivation for the crime. Lastly, the Bat Cave in Bronson Canyon was where the two had first met.

I sometimes wonder where my drive to find concrete answers to seemingly unsolvable mysteries comes from. Perhaps it began in my early childhood, which was a harrowing convergence of unpredictability and confusion consisting of the death of my father when I was two and the drug-and-alcohol-consumed life my mother used to lead. Or perhaps it is simply a pure fascination with human anatomy and scientific exploration. Regardless of its source, I intend to use my relentless curiosity and technological innovations to uncover truth everywhere I go.

Example 2: I am calling Mike a Seeker because he pursues knowledge and mastery in pursuit of a daunting goal he chooses for himself.

Male Seeker

Polyvinyl chloride: PVC. Infinite in function, this plastic is manipulated by man to serve his immensely diverse needs. It is the stone, the bronze, the iron of modern man.

I've always been intrigued by the mechanics of everyday objects. When I was three, I grimed up my hands while shifting the gears on my sister's new bicycle. When I was five, I snapped apart an alarm clock to examine the gears and wires that made the needles click in wonderful precision. When I was fourteen, I built an eight-foot wooden surfboard. In high school auto shop, I directed a team of students on a motorized bicycle build.

Another thrill of my childhood has been sailing. I loved the feeling of flying across a lake's surface and was amazed by the mechanics. I wanted to understand the sailboat, to get to know its every detail and feature that allowed it to catch the wind so efficiently and propel itself forward so effortlessly.

So I decided to build one. A sixteen-foot catamaran sailboat. In my backyard. Completely by myself. Completely from scratch. Out of PVC.

My project began with extensive research. After settling on a design that ingeniously used very large PVC irrigation pipes as the pontoons, I drew sketches, made lists of materials, and took the first of many trips to the hardware store.

Over the course of fourteen months, I became proficient on my new circular saw as I built a wooden deck, pontoon braces, and the centerboard. I ordered "dos tubos de unos 16 pies" as the Hispanic salesman—accustomed to supplying thousands of feet of pipe for acres of farmland—laughed. I built the mast, sail, jib, and boom, and as I aligned the ropes and stepped the mast, the giant wing that would propel my vessel filled with its first gust of air. I was now near the halfway point.

That's when I realized I had a major problem: my 300-pound wooden deck was too heavy for the available flotation. So I went back to the drafting board. After some thought, I decided that the most comfortable and cost-effective deck would be a light net, enforced with climbing webbing and stretched over braces across the pontoons. After a trip to the fabric and climbing supply stores, my mom gave me a short lesson on how to use our sewing machine.

Now as I cut and fit foam to finish the pontoons, wrap up the rudder controls, and polish the last bits of the boat, the maiden voyage draws closer and closer.

Building the catamaran sailboat has been the most difficult and rewarding project I've ever undertaken. Working from the initial idea and shaping it into its real form has challenged me to consider the technical, mechanical, and budgetary constraints before finding the best solution for each problem. It has also been a pursuit of pleasure, and I've loved every aspect of the process.

Throughout the fourteen months, I've managed my time between the demands of school, internships, jobs, volunteer work, and other extracurricular activities. I've also remained determined, even when those around me began to doubt me. But to say I built the boat alone without the help of people and resources around me would be a false statement. Without access to the Internet, my mom's sewing lesson, the advice of hardware store employees, and my dad's patience, I would not have been able to build the sailboat.

As I approach the end of this project, I realize I have confronted, embraced, and overcome real-world struggles that come with a real-world project. This project has taught me a lot, but it has especially taught me about myself. It has revealed and tested my curiosity, idealism, resilience, and self-motivation. And I know as soon as I get the boat out on its maiden voyage on open water, my mind will begin dreaming up my next project.

THE ADVENTURER: a slightly restless and deeply curious individualist who explores the world to find out who he/she is and seeks new experiences, joyful discovery, freedom, and authenticity with an open mind.

Example 1: I am calling Maddy an Adventurer because she embraces every new challenge with curiosity, enthusiasm, and an open mind while diving into a new setting to discover who she is.

Female Adventurer

In a society that champions individuals, I sometimes find myself searching for my place. Too often it seems the skills I have are not "trending" and the care with which I execute tasks goes unnoticed. However, last summer, while doing an internship at Boeing, I discovered my skills are both beautifully unique and unexpectedly valuable.

My first day on the Huntington Beach campus, the air is filled with power and possibility. But upon meeting the seventy-six other interns—all socially timid, exhaustingly high-achieving students who enthusiastically discuss microwave lengths for fun—I'm intimidated. "They are so different from me," I think. "How can I possibly fit in?"

Before starting at Boeing, I'd hoped to be placed in the Business Department. So when I'm assigned to IT Project Management, my heart sinks. I'm in a foreign place, surrounded by unfamiliar people, without the job I'd hoped for. However, as soon as I meet my mentor, we click. I see right away she's an active leader who loves people. She's just like me. And the adventure begins.

My main assignment during the internship is to reorganize the unpopular and visually boring website where employees share information. Eager and determined to improve it, I spend one whole day on Microsoft.com learning how to manipulate the site and another creating a new template. I add color, create folders, and even write a friendly user guide for the staff.

Outside IT, I join a project to help Boeing cut costs by evaluating which testing of materials can be safely eliminated. After researching materials and meeting with engineers to gain their seasoned input, I compile my findings and suggestions into a slideshow to be presented to the executive board.

At work, I bring my optimism to every task, collaboration, and interaction. Each day I put up a quote of the day in my cubicle, like Shakespeare's "We know what we are, but not what we may be." These draw people in and spark conversations as I offer inspiration and nurture a sense of community.

While at Boeing I also join a committee that plans events for the interns. I throw a fun beach party and find myself genuinely connecting to my peers. This proves to me that my skills fostering relationships are just as valuable as others' skills working on satellites and robots, easing my earlier concerns about belonging.

To close the internship, we are asked to create posters to describe our work. While others' are composed of computer screenshots and dry text, mine is a metaphorical image of a tree made up of project management vocabulary and Boeing executives' quotes about leadership. The night before the presentation, I bake 150 cupcakes decorated in Boeing blue and white. The next morning, I walk in knowing I'm different. Embracing who I am. Feeling proud.

My time at Boeing was a crazy whirlwind of new information, challenges, and personal growth. I loved meeting professionals who took time to talk with me, deeply appreciated their encouragement, and felt valued when the program director told me how glad he was to have my smile, warmth, and joy in the office.

This experience changed my perspective on myself. It taught me that I do and can fit in everywhere, and that I should value the unique skills I've been blessed with that allow me to strike up a conversation, learn from others, and find the best in people. It also helped me recognize that differences can be great assets as we all strive to learn, grow, and contribute.

Boeing's motto once was "Forever New Frontiers." And though my time there might not have inspired in me a desire to shoot rockets into space, it did succeed in inspiring me always to seek new frontiers where I can invest in what I am, explore what I may be, and encourage those around me as they do the same.

Example 2: I am calling Daniel an Adventurer because he independently and fearlessly explores the world to find himself.

Male Adventurer

I am unanchored. My parents, South Africans foreign to America, were forced to adapt by relying on themselves in an entirely new country. By doing so, they taught me to rely on myself as well. They raised me in an autonomous environment and allowed me freedom, offering me an extraordinary gift of independence. For me, this gift was thrilling. But it also raised the question: Am I worthy of such a legacy? What will I make of it? Where will I go?

A Day in Australia

With music playing in my earphones, I nervously find a seat on the bus and prepare for a three-hour ride. Having worked nonstop the last few weeks for my uncle's company in Sydney, Australia, I was given a day off while on a business trip with him. He had suggested I hang by the hotel pool, but I have a different idea. I plan to spend my time alone in Byron Bay, a landmark in my family's history. Just then, two women sporting backpacks step on the bus. My curiosity kicks in and I pull out my earphones to ask what they plan to do in Byron. I discover they are on their way to a music festival, and we are instantly launched into a passionate and lively discussion about the latest music in Australia and America.

My first view in Byron is of Julian Rocks, an outcrop protruding from the center of the bay. What is originally a fleeting thought immediately takes hold in my mind: scuba diving. An hour later, I am geared up on a small motorboat. Thrilled to discover that my dive mates are a group of teenagers from Spain, I fearlessly test out my high school Spanish on their forgiving ears. Finally, we reach the dive site. I put my faith in gravity and do a backward roll entry.

Once in the water, I exhale. I feel myself sink, almost to the bottom. I inhale. All restrictions placed on me by gravity have vanished; I am free to explore this entirely new world. Limitless opportunity with limited airtime. As I hover above the sea floor, I open my eyes. A red sea anemone harbors a clownfish on an iridescent reef bustling with commerce. Cleaner fish sweep the underbelly of a majestic manta ray as it glides into the deep blue. I scour dark trenches, determined to make discoveries.

When I resurface, I gratefully switch from tank to natural air as I crawl out of the frigid water and onto the boat. The engine kick starts and I wonder what I'll do next. My stomach decides for me.

Back in town, I find my way to The Balcony, a restaurant overlooking the bay. The menu is filled with exotic dishes, and I am reminded of the quirky South African meals my family eats at home. When my lunch arrives, food never tasted so good. Before I know it, I am rushing back to my bus.

When I think back on my day in Byron Bay, I am proud to discover the answer to my question about what I will do with my gift of independence. I am not afraid to face the unknown. I embrace life by seizing every opportunity and living in the moment. When given a single free day in a foreign country, I am not the guy who's going to sit by a hotel pool. I'm the guy who's going to venture out, seek new perspectives, pursue novel experiences, satisfy my needs, and find my way back. In my life, independence is not only a privilege, it is a passion.

For some people, growing up unanchored might sound frightening or unsettling. But for me, it has been exhilarating and inspiring. As I look ahead to college and beyond, I cannot wait to see where my gift will take me next.

THE REBEL: an outsider who revolts against what isn't working for him/herself or society and goes outside conventional behavior and morality to disrupt, change, and liberate.

Example 1: I am calling Miranda a Rebel because she fights against her school's rigid social rules, reaches across boundaries, and helps people find common ground.

Female Rebel

I am a high school anomaly. I spend my days with the intellectual kids, debating Faulkner's stylistic choices, finding the centripetal force of Earth, and joking about logarithms, integrals, and polar equations. But I spend my nights with the social kids, blasting music, making people laugh so hard they can't breathe, and leading chants in my school's Viking nation student section in support of my football player friends. Most of the time this works out okay. But this fall it didn't.

On the first day of school, I walked into my economics class and was surprised to find a mix of both the social and intellectual kids. I chose to sit next to my friends Josh and Jason, who are receivers on the football team. But every day, when asked to work in groups or discuss with partners, I felt torn because although I'm friends with both groups, they were not. The social kids called the intellectual kids weird, but I find that they attack challenges in ambitious and innovative ways. The intellectual kids called the social kids stupid, but I know that they are smart about different things, like relationships, sports strategies, and style.

While in the midst of this struggle of being caught between my different sets of friends, I read *One Flew over the Cuckoo's Nest* in AP Literature. In this novel, the main character, Randle Patrick McMurphy, is sent to a mental institution. While there, he realizes that most of the men are not crazy, they are just misunderstood, insecure, and controlled by the oppressive nurses and staff. He spends his time working against the nurse and showing the men how important it is to be an individual. In the end, McMurphy is killed, but he has made a difference on the ward because he taught the men not to conform. They begin to accept themselves and all of the other people around them for who they are.

I loved reading this book, and the message behind it has had a huge impact on me. This novel showed me that I must not fall into the monotony of conformity or let other people tell me how to live my life. It revealed to me that everyone is a unique individual and is special in his or her own way. It taught me how important it is to be myself and accept others for who they are.

After finishing the book, I did my best to bring McMurphy's lessons into my economics class and my life. I pulled Josh and Jason, the football players, into a group project with my intellectual friends and was thrilled to watch them actively engage and increase their understanding. And by using their knowledge of sports and professional athletes to predict the demand for a product that was endorsed by the New England Patriots, they introduced an entirely new perspective to our group. Also, I brought the intellectual kids to a football game. Although it was not their favorite thing, we all had fun together and they confessed that they were glad to cross this high school milestone off their bucket lists.

I am proud to be a high school anomaly. I am passionate about tolerance and inclusivity, and I believe that if you dig deep and care enough, you will be able to find something compelling about everyone you meet. By being friends and interacting with a lot of different types of people, I've learned to see things from many perspectives, which has increased my curiosity about and understanding of the world. As I look ahead to college, I can't wait to take chances, embrace opportunities, and push myself out of my comfort zone, all while being myself and encouraging others to do the same. Who knows?[36] With any luck, I might even become a college anomaly too![37]

Example 2: I am calling Austin a Rebel because when he was young he humorously went outside conventional behavior to innovate and succeed at business.

Male Rebel

I have always been passionate about business. Ever since I was five years old and my grandfather happily announced at a family dinner, "You know, Austin will make a great businessman when he grows up," I have been trying to prove him right. At five, I launched my business career by reselling items to my triplet brothers (often items that already belonged to them). Eventually, enough capital was raised, and I opened a lemonade stand. Right away, I noticed a trend that when my younger sister was with me, the stand sold more lemonade. To put my theory to the test, we separated. When she sold more cups than I did, I made the executive decision to hire her as a full-time employee, and profits skyrocketed. Later that year, my father

---

36   Note how powerful a tiny addition like "Who knows?" can be. It instantly humanizes the writer and helps her connect to the reader. If you have an opportunity to conversationally reach out to your reader, seize it.

37   Note how the writer **circled back**: she opened by confessing she is a high school anomaly and closed by hoping to become a college anomaly too.

opened a stock market account for me. At the beginning, it was just for me to learn about investing. However, at age seven, I gradually took over the reins. In my eleven years of investing, I have doubled my investment three times.

While at school, I launched other ventures, like trading for better lunches. I would beg my mother to buy Snack Packs because they had great value: for one Snack Pack, I could get a whole Lunchables. Also, because I played a lot of basketball, I developed a love of basketball sneakers, and at age twelve I started an eBay business buying and selling them. To this day, I still have a 100 percent feedback rating. In junior high, after the iPhone was launched, I started an iPhone customization, fix, and jailbreak company. When I changed schools for high school, my business expanded because I now had two markets in which to offer my services.

Investing in the market, or at least checking my portfolio, is something I do daily. My love for investing has inspired me, along with a few friends, to start the Loyola Investment Club. Last year, I was elected president by the 65 registered members. This year, I was reelected by the 150 registered members. And we now have 270 students participating in our annual Loyola Stock Game.

This past summer, I attended USC's Exploring Entrepreneurship Program and had the opportunity to test my business aptitude. The sensational four-week program was rigorous and rewarding. For the final project, I gave a presentation about an original business idea I had engineered with three teammates to market to potential investors. We pitched to professors and actual investors who were brought in to give us real-time feedback. Our idea, Kosher Kravings, was for a kosher food truck company in New York City and Los Angeles, the second and third largest Jewish population centers in the world. When we did our initial research, we were surprised to discover that nothing like this exists in either market. Our team recognized that it offered the perfect opportunity to capture a niche in the marketplace.

While at the program, I loved being in a community of peers who were also passionate about business, eager to challenge themselves, and mostly unafraid to speak in public. I hope to attend a college that has a similar environment. I also greatly appreciated the opportunity to test my growing business skills on a much larger scale. At the end of class, I was proud to learn that my team won the Best Final Presentation Award, and I personally had received an A.

As a person with diagnosed learning disabilities, I was delighted to find that if I truly love a topic, I can focus, learn, grow, and succeed. When I look back on my life, I realize that business is in my genes; it's in my blood. It has helped mold me into a curious, personable, and determined young adult who is excited to work hard, prosper, and give back to my community.

THE DREAMER: **an innocent who seeks happiness and fulfillment through faith, hope, and optimism; desires simplicity and goodness; finds renewal in nature; and is calm, a bit naïve, and positive.**

Example 1: I am calling Arielle a Dreamer because she works to inspire hope.

Female Dreamer

My job is listener. Although most people think support lines exist to give advice, they don't. It's against the rules. Essentially, I just listen.

In tenth grade, I discovered Teen Line, a hotline that teenagers can call to talk about anything going on in their lives. Never having heard of Teen Line or anything like it, I was surprised that it even existed. A place for teens to call in to other teens to talk about issues that were mutually relatable sounded exciting and intriguing and like something I definitely wanted to be involved in. After filling out the extensive application and going to my individual and group interviews, I was thrilled to learn that I had been accepted.

During my three-month training, my group met three times a week. Initially I felt overwhelmingly timid, but I ignored my shyness and focused on my ambition to get on the phone. We began by learning how to talk to teens. We learned to empathize, to normalize a caller's feelings, and to reflect feelings so the caller knew someone could hear them. We learned the basics of how to take a call and did role-plays on fifteen different topics, including pregnancy, runaways, relationships, self-harm, substance abuse, suicide, and child abuse. Finally, I was faced with my listener's test, a practice call with an intense scenario of feelings and events such as rape, suicide, and self-harm all at once. After passing the test, I must've smiled for days.

My first official shifts as a listener at Teen Line were filled with anticipation and nervousness. During the early weeks, I received many prank calls. But over time, I also began to receive real calls for help. Most commonly, I would talk to teens upset with their friends, parents, boyfriends or girlfriends. One night, while on a text shift, I talked to Jenny. She was a thirteen-year old girl who was depressed, being bullied, cutting herself daily, and crying herself to sleep. I tried to help her understand that what she was feeling was understandable considering all that she was going through, and I tried to help her identify supports in her life. Toward the end of our text, Jenny said she had to go, but I urged her to call back when she felt ready to talk. Before hanging up, she sent me, "Thank you. I love you so much. You really helped me a lot." That night, for the first time, I felt like I had done something of importance and had really helped someone in need.

Reflecting on my experience at Teen Line, I am surprised to realize how comforting and soothing I find each shift. Working on a hotline takes me away from my own concerns. It allows me to focus on how I can best support others, and I always leave feeling better than when I arrived. Working at Teen Line, I've discovered that when a person tells me something they've never told anyone else, I feel an enormous sense of privilege and responsibility. Taking these calls, I have admired these teens who are struggling but not giving up.

When my mom was nearly a teen, her father— the grandfather I never met—committed suicide. As I think of how alone he and my mom must have felt, I feel simultaneously sad and inspired. By working on Teen Line, and by trying to be a good friend when I am not at Teen Line, I know now that we do not have to be alone. I am a person who likes to connect. Over the past year, I have grown out of my shyness and have come to realize that if we are willing to reach out to others, and if we are willing to reach back when others reach out to us, we can create a stronger, more compassionate community together. That's a community I want to help build.

Example 2: I am calling Maxwell a Dreamer because he seeks happiness and fulfillment in the bounty of nature.

Male Dreamer

Onions, tomatoes, lettuce, celery, cabbage, broccoli, kale, cauliflower, Swiss chard, beets, carrots, turnips, potatoes, peas, beans, summer squash, winter squash, spinach, strawberries, and pumpkins.

Three years ago, my father and I took a chainsaw to the ficus hedge in our front yard to make room for a garden. We built a large raised bed, laid chicken wire on the bottom, and brought in irrigation. This was the second vegetable garden I ever had, and through much trial and even more error, it eventually became quite successful.

A year later, I came upon a book called *The New Victory Garden* by the late Bob Thomson. Thomson's practice of starting his seedlings indoors with special lights and heating pads inspired me to try the same. I built an indoor greenhouse for starting seedlings in the garage. In time, I became more independent and hardly had to purchase any plants at nurseries.

One year, my family visited Thomas Jefferson's Monticello in Virginia. There, I discovered that Jefferson was a botanist who cultivated 330 species of plants, was a meticulous record keeper, and kept a diary with observations of his plants. Jefferson and Thomson have taught me to keep records of my own seedlings and their early development.

Although I'm a good-natured person, I have fought many foes inside my garden. When aphids descended on my cabbages, I sprayed them with organic repellents. When snails ate my lettuce, I enticed them into dishes of beer, where they drowned. When squirrels munched my new beet sprouts, I baited them with peanuts, trapped them in cages, and released them in the nearby wilderness. But of all the foes my gardening has forced me to face, the ultimate one has been my own shyness and reserve.

After running a car washing business for a few years, I wanted to start a retail business selling my seedlings at my local farmers market. Though I was nervous about interacting with customers, I decided to give it a try.

Early one Sunday morning, I brought eight plastic cell packs filled with pea seedlings to the farmer's market. I set up my folding plastic table and displayed typed instructions for the care of the plants. I was ready to sell, but no one stopped by. I realized that if I wanted to attract business, I couldn't be passive. I'd have to flag people down and lure them in.

Over time, I learned to stand out in front of my table and call out, "Vegetable seedlings for sale!" Not only did I feel like the man from one of my favorite childhood books, *Caps for Sale*, but I drew in customers. I learned to be more outgoing, traded growing tips, adapted to the market, and grew my business. Like Jefferson, I learned to be disciplined about keeping records and documented my sales data, which I later analyzed. And I almost always reinvested my earnings in my garden.

Coaxing seeds into plants has been crucial to my understanding of how miraculous and precious life is. I observe how each plant matures in its unique way, its imperfections part of its nature. I find a sacred lesson in each harvest that teaches me to try different practices and take note of what went wrong so I can improve the following season. Gardening has taught me to meet all of my challenges with patience, perseverance, curiosity, hard work, flexibility, joy, and a willingness to dig in.

In 1811, Thomas Jefferson wrote to Charles Willson Peale about his garden. He found beauty and insight in "the failure of one thing repaired by the success of another" over seasons and time.

I also find beauty and insight in my own failures and successes, and I feel grateful for the sharp and shiny tools that gardening has given me. I can't wait to see what I cultivate with them next year on new ground.

THE CAREGIVER: **a nurturer who has a passion to help, comfort, and protect others from harm; is filled with compassion and generosity; and has concern for others and the larger world.**

Example 1: I am calling Lauren a Caregiver because she learns to be compassionate and caring, and she generously wants to share that with others.

Female Caregiver

All my life, I thought it was good to be private. Sure, the majority of the time I was playful and funny and outgoing, but whenever anything difficult came along, I kept it to myself. I thought it was easier—better—not to open up. But I was wrong.

During Thanksgiving of my junior year of high school, my older brother, who was home from his freshman year of college, had a breakdown that was triggered by drug use. After being hospitalized at UCLA, he was transferred to rehab for substance abuse. While my brother was in treatment, my parents would visit him constantly. But I stayed home, lost, confused, worried, overwhelmed, too afraid to go see him. While my grades slipped and I struggled to stay focused on school, I told no one about what was going on.

A couple months later, my brother came home from rehab. At first, everyone was tense. I wasn't sure who he was anymore or what to say to him. After being close when we were younger, we had grown apart.

But, slowly, we began to talk. He told me everything he had gone through, and I realized how much he had hidden from us. I wanted to support him, wanted to help him break down the walls he had built around himself. I wanted to reach through the walls I had silently and unknowingly been building around myself but was unsure how. I discovered the best way was by just being there, sitting and watching TV together, even though in silence, I felt present and connected to him.

Over time, we opened up to each other, shared our struggles, built trust, and grew closer than ever. Our relationship changed, and we started to check in with each other and seek each other's input. We got more comfortable with one another because there were no longer any secrets. I learned how to stay open and accept him. I discovered how much he means to me and showed him how much I care for him.

As my brother came out of his shell, I realized I needed to push myself out of my own shell. I wanted to take what I learned from him out into the rest of my life. So, after ten months of keeping my story secret, I finally told my school counselor and three best friends what happened with my brother. At first, I didn't know how they would react. I feared they might judge my family or me. But they were all supportive and loving, wanting only to help, and I felt a huge sense of relief. I discovered that it's actually easier and better to be open and not have secrets. I learned that I can trust people and let them in.

When I reflect on the past year, I am proud of many things: my strength and courage, my ability to maintain composure and be the rock that my family needed, my willingness—despite fear—to stay present with my brother, and my new understanding that it is better to be open and truly connected to others than closed and alone. As I look ahead to college, I feel a new sense of confidence and excitement for the eye-opening journey ahead, one that I hope will be filled with adventure and discovery and the thrilling pursuit of knowledge. I know I will face challenges, but I also know I will be able to handle them and keep them in perspective. Because I have torn down the walls around myself, I know how to reach out to others. And if I see my peers struggling down a lonely path, I will be the person to reach out to them, because I have gone down that path, and I have learned the way back.

Example 2: I am calling Jacob a Caregiver because he digs deep to make a difference in others' lives.

Male Caregiver

It's a cool summer night and the eight- and nine-year-olds I coach in a nonprofit soccer program run by the LAPD start to warm up. As they begin their usual goofy chatter, I turn my attention to the starting goalkeeper, who is on his belly, actively avoiding any physical activity whatsoever. It's the same start to every practice with Walter. It takes me five minutes just to get him up off the ground. Watching him, I grow upset, knowing that he's wasting this opportunity to become a better player. What can I possibly do or say to make a difference in this kid's life?

I had a coach who made a difference in mine. When I entered my high school soccer program as a freshman, I met coach Darren Davies, who was a very funny, very competitive man in his early 30s. He was different from any other coach I had played for before. He never told me to go out on the field and perform a drill; he went out on the field with me and showed me how. During the summer going into my sophomore year, Darren had the trust and faith in me to promote me from the freshman team straight to varsity. A month later, he shared the news that I would start for the varsity team. His confidence in me filled me with confidence in myself.

Coach Darren taught me many valuable lessons. During my freshman year, I received five yellow cards for fouls, retaliation, and yelling at the ref. Under Darren's guidance, I learned not to let any beef with other players, or my short-term frustration, get in the way of winning the game. As a result, sophomore and junior years I got no yellow cards. At a tournament after a loss, when my teammates and I started to trash-talk opposing players, Coach Darren kept us in line. I learned that even when emotions run high, I have to be disciplined and remain a good sport. When we beat a tough team, I learned to be proud of myself. When we lost to an easy team, I learned to look at myself in the mirror and think about what I could do differently next time. Coach Darren taught us to respect our opponents. He inspired me to make better choices.

One day, at early morning practice before school, the head of my soccer program called us all in before we started to warm up. Our team knew something was wrong, but we had no idea what it was. Then he delivered news that would change my life forever. The night before, Darren had suffered a fatal heart attack. I remember not being able to breathe. Then I just broke down.

How could a healthy soccer coach just die all of a sudden? It didn't make sense. I was mad, shocked, and just so sad. How could someone who affected me so deeply on a daily basis just exit right out of my life?

Back on that cool summer night, as I wait for Walter to get up from the ground, I suddenly realize what I must do: I must take everything I learned from Coach Darren and teach it to Walter. I must set an example for him, reach out to him, make a commitment to him and see it through, and teach him the skills the way Coach Darren taught them to me. In life, Coach Darren taught me to strive to be a better person on and off the soccer field. In death, he taught me that I might not have a tomorrow, so I should start to make a difference today. I plan to passionately carry that lesson with me into every day of my future and try to positively impact as many people as I can. In that way, I can keep his spirit alive. [38]

---

38 This essay offers a successful example of a student who wrote about another person's death but kept the focus on himself. It never falls into the trap of becoming a eulogy for Coach Darren; instead, it wisely remains focused on how the writer lives his life given Coach Darren's influence.

THE ARTIST: an innovator who uses imagination and creativity to bring beauty, culture, and form to the world; a nonconformist who loves to express him/herself and bring his/her vision to life.

Example 1: I am calling Lulu an Artist because she takes photos to passionately and creatively explore the world around her.

Female Artist

EL CERRITO STEEL AND CO. blares across the metal building, juxtaposed against the blue, five-o'clock sky. Click. I notice that the warehouse is made up of three distinct textures, all different colors. Click. I spin in my Converse to confront the graffitied train tracks in my viewfinder. Click. Satisfied, I climb back into my father's car and think to my thirteen-year-old self, "I'm going to see it all."

Shortly after receiving my first camera, I began to document everything in my immediate environment. Sitting on my front steps, I watched cyclists and motorists zoom by while crows lazily composed themselves atop telephone wires. Later, my fascination with people took hold. Enamored of the idea of preserving authenticity in an art form, I began to understand those around me on a deeper level through the photos they helped me create. My camera became an extension of my body.

Now, walking through the world, I am drawn to color and vibrancy. A person with bright red hair. A green neon sign. A purple handbag swinging off a woman's arm. These details make me feel more engaged, more present. Last winter, after a seven-year drought had rendered the local landscape brown and lifeless, an El Niño left the plants healthy and the rain spurred me into action. I dragged my friends to the Marin Headlands, camera in hand, seeking stimulation. Running down the trail, I felt the emerald and forest green hues practically seep into my skin.

Taking photographs and exploring my environment has propelled me into a cycle of discovery. Traveling all over the Bay Area in search of varied landscapes has transformed me. In San Francisco, where most see a city teeming with stories of urban success, I see those of displacement and gentrification as well. Commuting ten minutes from my comfortable East Bay town to Richmond, I see dilapidated houses, scarred neighborhoods, and plumes of smoke from the local refinery that stand as symbols of stark inequality.

One day, while riding a BART train with a friend, my teacher's assignment reverberates in my mind. Fast shutter for bright situations. Slow shutter speed once the sun sets. Suddenly, an image is projected in front of me, and I know where we must go.

From the station we hurry to the bus bound for Ocean Beach. As we approach the water, the sky becomes a palette of pinks and oranges. Giddy at the sight of the turbulent water and vivid colors, I convince my friend to sit in the chaotic foam and swirls of the ocean. I plunge my tripod into the water and press the shutter button. This time there is no instant click. The sensor has to take in ten seconds of data, movement, and image. I look down at the display where my friend is calm, seemingly frozen in a torrent of motion. The roaring of the sea fades away and all I can take in is my friend steadfast in her place amid the ocean's immense, natural power.

A week later I receive my grade and see a note attached from my teacher. "Lulu, You have much to offer other young photographers who are learning their craft. You have much to offer the world, which is still learning how to see."

Documenting and creating photographs is what I'm most proud of. Seeking out unique images has taught me to be an active participant in my world and helped me pursue beauty and truth in the subjects I capture. The resulting images and relationships have the potential to humanize sometimes broad and colorless stories, effect real change, or simply move and connect us to each other and to nature. Moving forward, I can't wait to discover new colors, landscapes, and experiences, explore the role of art in life, and use my insights to inspire and mobilize.

Example 2: I am calling Rob an Artist because he makes films to explore and express what authentically matters to him.

Male Artist

As the lights dim over the heads of my thirty classmates and several pensive instructors, I begin to quake in anticipation. I had been assigned to create an abstract documentation of a physical space and for the last several days had been working to form something that would astound my fellow filmmakers and teachers alike. However, in the darkness of the classroom, my heart sinks as I realize that I am the only one impressed by my abstract interpretation of the campus parking lot. In my half-baked attempt to become the next Luis Buñuel, I lost something fundamentally important: authenticity.

Last summer, I was one of only thirty applicants selected from 350 to embark on an intensive, four-week film program at the California State Summer School for the Arts. I stayed on the CalArts campus with a select group of aspiring, ambitious artists while taking part in a concentrated filmmaking course. In the mornings, I learned the fundamentals: sound production, art direction, equipment, film analysis, and the behemoth that is editing. In the afternoons and evenings, I wrote and shot short films based on various assigned topics. Late into the nights, I edited to meet impending deadlines.

With the failure of my first short film, I realized that to excel in this program I needed to pursue my own interests and artistic visions instead of focusing on how I was perceived by those around me. As a result, my second and third projects improved. For our final assignment—a documentary accurately portraying the life of someone on campus—I vowed to draw inspiration from a more emotional and visceral place.

While at CSSSA, I had become close with my roommate. Gabe was an open, lively, passionate visual artist and was the perfect subject for my documentary. He easily accepted his own distinct attributes and never conformed to those around him. However, he also confessed to me that he was constantly struggling with the fluid nature of his sexuality. I decided that the complex emotions that surround sexuality and often transcend linguistic expression would be perfect to explore in my documentary.

For the next few days, I interviewed Gabe and filmed him as he talked, danced, and shared his paintings. As I began editing my project, I pulled in various elements of B-roll footage to expose parallels and embellish contrasts to his dialogue. For example, when Gabe described making out with a girl purely because of the societal expectations that men face, I matched his speech with a clip from an 80s film of two high school lovers passionately kissing. After editing for two full days, I finally showed my film to the department. When the screen went dark and the lights rose once again, I was happily greeted with applause and admiration. However, what made me most pleased was the satisfaction that came from knowing that I had committed to something that deeply mattered to me.

All of my life, I have aspired to be an individual. As part of a humanities magnet high school, I am constantly trying to derive meaning from the various philosophical texts we read and apply them to my experiences in hopes of understanding my life as a human being. From my unparalleled experience at CSSSA and throughout my education, I have discovered that the best way to grow as an individual and truly become content is to create things from my own passions. No longer can I be swayed by the manipulative powers of the Other, or how one perceives the Other for that matter. My true north will be my intuition, inspired by genuine curiosity and challenged by critical thinking. And even if my efforts don't succeed, I know now I can always find meaning in the striving.

THE LEADER: a role model who takes control to lead a group to success and prosperity; acts with an innate authority that makes others want to follow; takes responsibility for making life stable; and reinforces order.

Example 1: I am calling Izabella a Leader because she rallies her peers to create something moving and spectacular and greater than what they could each create individually.

Female Leader

A cacophony of sounds emanates from the black box theater. Inside, the atmosphere is frenzied as forty wildly diverse students attempt to prepare for our impending show. Actors miss entrance cues. Costumes droop. Musicians play out-of-tune instruments. A reverberating echo comes from the soundboard. And backstage, everyone is afraid to go near the hair station because someone has lice. When the music and theater teachers are called away by a student emergency, they leave me in charge of this entire tech rehearsal. How did I get here?

When I was ten, I learned how to play the clarinet. In junior high, I loved music and participating in the concert and jazz bands so much that I taught myself to play the saxophone. But when I began high school, there were fewer instrumental opportunities available, so I sought out other creative outlets. As a sophomore, I took a photography class, where I created the poster for the fall drama production and developed a close relationship with the theater teacher. She encouraged me to get involved in the behind-the-scenes aspects of our school performances, and I happily took on greater and greater responsibilities. The next year, when my school decided to put on a musical production of Shakespeare's *Much Ado About Nothing* and my teacher offered me—a junior—the job of assistant director, I was both thrilled and nervous.

The school's version of the play was to be set in 1940s WWII Sicily, so my initial task was to research key design aspects necessary to mount the show. I dove into researching what American soldiers and Big Band performers wore during that era and looked for specific historical figures who might capture the play's characters' personalities, like using Rosie the Riveter as inspiration for Beatrice. I stayed up late watching old black-and-white movies to discover period hair and makeup styles. Because our play would be a musical, I listened to a hundred different swing songs and chose two for the big dance numbers that would bookend the show. We brainstormed inventive ways to integrate dancers and choreography with the music, like casting a trio to perform as the Andrews Sisters. While directing the actors, I was captivated as we experimented with new ways to help the actors express various emotions.

Although my learning curve was enormous, I grew into my leadership role and actively problem-solved. When we had more actors than available roles, I suggested double casting parts so more students could participate. When I was bombarded daily with endless questions, I learned to be decisive. When students lost focus, I coaxed them back on track. When cast mates argued, I put on my peace negotiator's hat. When the lice problem occurred, I kept the student's identity confidential. When we neared the performance date and realized that the stage thrust left too little room for our audience, I suggested seating some brave audience members on the catwalk. For every problem that arose, I tried to innovate a solution. Every day was different, and most were not easy.

But as I stood there in the middle of that tech rehearsal, days before our premiere, engulfed in turmoil and uncertainty, I realized something amazing: instead of panicked, I felt empowered. I had learned that ambitious pursuits require hard work and creative risks, but they also lead to spectacular results. And, as a member of a troupe,

I had discovered that we are capable of producing something in collaboration that is so much more imaginative than that which we can accomplish alone.

Today, as I look forward to college, I feel ready and eager to join my new community as we step together onto our next stage.

Example 2: I am calling Andrew a Leader because he captains his lacrosse team with unusual sensitivity and thoughtfulness.[39]

Male Leader

Weathered, beat up, an octagonal stick with a sandpapery feel. Six feet tall, like me, but with a stiff white scoop and malleable net. Just holding it fills me with adrenaline and joy.

Some of my happiest moments have been while playing lacrosse. I love the sport's athleticism, skill, and nuance, and when I joined my high school team as a freshman, I couldn't have been more excited. Yet, freshman year was overshadowed by our team's seniors, who disregarded the underclassman and were notorious for their use of drugs and alcohol. This made it difficult to follow their leadership.

Sophomore year I earned a starting spot on

39 Note that just because you are a Leader it doesn't mean you have to walk around behaving presidential. This lacrosse team captain leads with his humor, warmth, and humanity.

the varsity defense, and I was both thrilled and terrified to play with and against bigger and more experienced players. However, this year's seniors were the nicest group of guys who generously guided underclassmen on the field and happily included us in activities off the field.

Junior year, when I was named one of two varsity captains, I had to stretch my playful, chill nature to assume huge responsibilities. Right away I vowed to teach and mentor the underclassmen. When a sophomore started vaping, I expressed my concerns. When a freshman's father passed away, I sat with him at lunch and drove him home from practice every day. As a leader, I strived to make the season fun for everyone.

In ten years of playing lacrosse, I've had only one experience that made me question my love for the game. Sophomore year, my team traveled to Colorado to play the top ranked team in the West. When we came up short, I was bummed, but I felt optimistic that my performance was improving and happy to be with friends. On our way to the bus, my coach overheard me laughing and commented, "I guess you don't care. And since you don't care, you won't mind being benched for the next game." Hearing those words hurt me deeply and caused tears to well up in my eyes. It made me wonder if there was a place on the team for a dedicated yet laid-back player like me.

When we returned from Colorado, I tried to be serious and focused at practice. I didn't laugh or mess around. As a result, I didn't feel like myself, and I didn't play well. One day, my coach grew frustrated and kicked me out of practice. I felt so confused. I didn't know what he wanted or who I should be. Worst of all, I'd lost sight of why I was even playing. Finally, I asked my coach to sit down and talk. I made him understand that while our personalities differed—he was an intense guy who didn't let losses go, while I was an easygoing guy who learned from mistakes and moved on—I also passionately wanted to succeed. From that point forward, everything improved. I returned to my old self, started having fun again, and played the best I'd ever played. By the end of the season, our team made it to the championship, and my coach and I reached a mutual understanding.

Lacrosse has offered me the tightest brotherhood I've ever known. It's inspired in me a relentless discipline, outrageous joy, and dedication to working toward collective goals, treating all people with respect, and having a positive impact. But the most important lesson I've learned has also been the most unexpected one: to stay true to myself. Playing lacrosse has challenged me to think about who I am and how and why I do things. It's revealed that to make a difference in my community, it's not enough to share my physical abilities and intense work ethic. I must also share my humanity: my unique personality, kindness, humor, and desire to connect, support, and have fun with everyone. Learning this lesson hasn't always been easy, but mastering it has allowed me to be me.

ANOTHER UNIQUE POINT OF VIEW

Just as Josh's essay about doing good was about a motivating theme in his life (rather than a single event or interest), the following essay is about an attitude that colors writer Zianna's life everywhere she goes. Zianna was answering the Common App prompt "Describe a place or environment where you are perfectly content." Her answer was unconventional. Instead of wanting to choose a single place, she insisted she felt most content while out exploring the world. She wanted her essay to be a dynamic collage of how she engages at lots of places—her school, work, volunteer gig, summer internship, and hometown of Los Angeles. When she couldn't figure out how to open and close her essay, I asked her, "What is the most joyful moment you can remember while being out in the world?" Instantly, she knew just where to begin and end.

Zianna's Common App Essay

I'm sitting in the Hollywood Bowl with my most adventurous friend and 18,000 other Angelenos, waiting for Edward Sharpe and the Magnetic Zeros to come onstage. People balance their picnic dinners on their laps, make friends, and share tips on exciting new music and bands. I can truly feel the energy in the audience. The lights finally dim and I join the cheering in anticipation of the main act. Although I know only one person in the entire crowd, in this moment I feel wonderfully connected to the thousands of jubilant strangers surrounding me. As the lights start to come up on stage, I ask myself, where else have I felt this joyful, this engaged, this content?

Last year, in my US History class, I felt wonderfully challenged and hugely captivated. My teacher encouraged conversation rather than cramming. My classmates and I had the freedom and time to explore many aspects of different historical events and figures, like the Triangle Shirtwaist Factory fire and the Tuskegee Airmen. We shared ideas, challenged assumptions, exchanged heated debate, and learned from each other. We brought the history to life.

When I am not at school, I count myself lucky to work at a neighborhood boutique where I have taken on big responsibilities: opening and closing the store, helping with the website and social networking, buying merchandise, and even painting the store's much anticipated annual Christmas mural. Yet, the most valuable thing that my time at the boutique has taught me is how to create a community. I have learned from the store's generous owner to appreciate interactions between people, share stories, and make everyone feel welcome. I'm moved by the diversity of the customers who make their way to the register. And I have embraced the idea that allowing people to surprise me makes life richer.

Nowhere am I more surprised than at a special education preschool where I volunteer. I help the kids eat, walk, and play, and I get drooled on, bitten, and hit. But I'm not deterred, because I have learned so much from them: simplicity, humor, living in the moment, and that people are people regardless of their limitations. They teach me resilience, gratitude, and to be happy with what I have. Every time I visit this place, I leave it a better person.

Last summer I learned an unexpected lesson while I shadowed an orthopedic surgeon in his office for three weeks. While I expected to be impressed by his advanced skills giving cortisone injections, draining flooded hips, and removing staples, what I did not expect was to be most moved by his gentle care. He taught me that helping people takes both passion and compassion.

Some of my very happiest moments happen on the weekends while exploring Los Angeles—I drag my friends out to hike Fryman Canyon; ride the Metro; visit MOCA, the Science Center, Chinatown; and ride the Ferris wheel overlooking the Pacific Ocean on the Santa Monica Pier. Each adventure offers me an opportunity to explore an unfamiliar place, discover a new point of view, make a connection, and reflect on how I want to live.

Back at the Hollywood Bowl, as the band jams and the crowd rocks, I realize that I am most content when I am out in the world, fearlessly exploring new environments and joyfully learning from others. I passionately believe that I have something meaningful to learn everywhere I go and from everyone I meet. I know that I will always be eager to challenge myself, seize every opportunity, and stretch my heart and mind to be open to all that the world has to offer. And with this realization, the music fills me, and I get up on my feet and dance.[40]

Zianna used the concert at the Hollywood Bowl to open her essay and draw in her reader. At the end of her opening paragraph, she posed a question (where else have I felt this content?), which catapulted the reader into the essay's body in which she illustrated her own joyful engagement. When she reached the closing paragraph, she returned to the Hollywood Bowl and answered her own

---

40 The building blocks of Zianna's essay:
Five Best-Day Words: creative, present, engaged, curious, joyful
Story: actively exploring her world
Message: I strive to learn something everywhere I go and from everyone I meet.
Archetypes: Artist, Seeker, Dreamer

question. Zianna's Unique Point of View—her openness and passion to learn all she can everywhere she goes and from everyone she meets—is impressive and extremely moving. And it clearly shows how she will make the most of all that college has to offer.

SAME TOPIC, DIFFERENT RESULT

To see an essay very different from the one Cole wrote about working at the pizza parlor, take a look at what Fiona wrote about working at Starbucks. Where Cole's descriptions were comic and light, Fiona's—while still being youthful—are more sober and thoughtful as she observes and reflects on broader social issues. Note how she opens with unexpected intellectual vitality and thematically connects what she learns to how she lives. I particularly love this essay because it reveals her maturing compassion and critical thinking. After reading this, it's clear that any college would be lucky to call this diligent, empathetic student one of its own.

Fiona's Common App Essay

In chemistry class, I learned to determine a carbon dioxide molecule's polarity by looking at the differences in the electronegativity values of the molecule's elements. If the difference falls between 0.4 and 1.7, the molecule is polar. For carbon dioxide, the difference is 1.2, so I assumed it is polar. But when I investigated further and actually drew out the Lewis dot structures, I saw the dipole and symmetry of the bonds, which revealed that the molecule is actually nonpolar.

In chemistry, I learned it is not a good idea to make assumptions about polarities. In life, I learned it is not a good idea to make assumptions about people.

The summer before my junior year, I got my first job as a Starbucks barista. At first, it was terrifying. How was I supposed to memorize all the drinks, get the regulars' orders down, and know that iced coffee stays fresh two hours longer than iced tea? Scariest of all, how was I supposed to relate to my coworkers, all of whom were older and had much more life experience? Early that summer, I questioned why I even got the job. After about a month, however, I learned to love it.

Working at Starbucks taught me independence and accountability. To land the job, I handled the application process, two interviews, and even the tax forms on my own. Once hired, I was the one who got myself to my 4 a.m. shifts, and I was the one who sometimes worked until 11 p.m.

Before I got the job, I'd always assumed that people working at Starbucks were not very educated. Once I started working there, I discovered how wrong I was when a coworker finished the *New York Times* crossword puzzle during his lunch break. I soon learned I was working with a woman who was fluent in Hindi and was supporting her daughter through Harvard. And one day when I complained about my chemistry final, my 35-year-old shift supervisor who was back in college announced, "I have a chem final too!"

Though my coworkers and I all took separate paths to our green aprons, come opening time, none of our differences matter. While hustling through our hectic Sunday shift, we are like an eight-armed humming machine, working together to warm muffins, steam milk, and blend Frappuccinos. When the person making drinks gets overwhelmed, someone slides over to help. When the smiling face at the register can barely smile anymore, someone steps up and relieves her.

My store is in Santa Monica on Wilshire Boulevard, a border between the two sides of the city. The affluent north side is where celebrities and movie producers live. The modest south side is where teachers and blue-collar workers reside. Due to this location, our store serves a wide variety of customers. We have the regular who once gave me $50 for my college fund, and we have the homeless man to whom we give a free coffee almost every day (don't tell corporate!).

Working at Starbucks has opened my eyes and made me more mindful of the community around me. I know now that I can't assume a customer speaks English, has money in his pocket, or will treat me like anything other than a coffee-serving robot. So I've learned to respond with my best high school Spanish, my greatest compassion, and plenty of patience.

Just as I am proud to have learned not to make assumptions about a molecule's polarity, I am even prouder to no longer make assumptions about people. I feel grateful to have learned that life is richer when we meet everyone with mutual respect and understanding. And I can't wait to take these lessons to college, where I will arrive with an open mind, a curiosity about others, and the wisdom always to tip my barista well.[41]

Remember, an essay about working at Starbucks is not really about working at Starbucks. It's about the challenges confronted and larger lessons learned while in a particular setting, and it's about the writer's unique sensitivity and voice. Imagine if Cole worked alongside Fiona at Starbucks and then wrote an essay about his job. Because of his different attitude and nature, his essay would look and sound nothing like hers. Same job, very different people, vastly different resulting essays.

---

41   The building blocks of Fiona's essay:
Five Best-Day Words: independent, ambitious, open-minded, friendly, compassionate
Story: working at Starbucks
Message: I am a person who meets everyone I encounter with respect and curiosity.
Archetypes: Seeker, Leader, Adventurer

ART SCHOOL

If you are applying to art school, make sure your personal statement establishes your creative track record, illustrates your work ethic, and conveys your passion. When you read Andreas's essay below, you'll get a glimpse into why he got into every school he applied to.

Andreas's Common App Essay

For as long as I can remember, I've longed to be part of the world of animation. I want to dedicate my life's work to bringing ideas, characters, and stories to life. Everywhere I go and everything I see provides inspiration for fantastical characters, never-imagined universes, and untold stories. When I draw, I express my individuality in the way I see and portray things. When I animate, I am set free from the limits of the natural world and the laws of physics. All I need are my imagination, personal experience, training, and 10,000 hours. This last piece I'm working on every day.

I've been drawing since I could hold a pencil. At seven, I learned stop motion and took my first animation class. I spent the next eight years making flip books and animating digitally in Adobe Flash (2D). At fifteen, I enrolled in the New York Film Academy's summer animation program, where I worked ten hours a day, five days a week learning 3D animation. At sixteen and seventeen, I taught computer animation to kids. During my current gap year, I am studying art and animation to gain the skills I will need to succeed as a computer artist.

I am currently taking graphite/charcoal figure drawing and computer animation classes for four hours per day, five days per week. I've never been more challenged or frustrated. I've never made more mistakes. And I've never been happier.

In class, I focus on anatomical accuracy, varied values of light to dark, and gestural lines that capture weight and motion. My style is refined, as I prefer soft lines. In all of my classes, I am the youngest student, sometimes by as many as forty years. I especially enjoy receiving critical feedback and advice from instructors. When the teacher is busy with other students, class members rely on each other for help. I've learned to depend on my classmates for guidance and feel great when they seek me out for assistance.

Without a doubt, I genuinely enjoy drawing subjects that are visually interesting instead of aesthetically beautiful. In class, drawing a muscular model lacks the challenge of visualizing underlying muscular landmarks. For interest's sake, I'll take a fat, hairy slob over a Calvin Klein model any day.

I am proud to have arrived in a place where discipline is the driving force in every aspect of my life, including art. I no longer wait for motivation to draw. I work. And I've learned that my best pieces are the result of both effort and perseverance.

I love animation because it is the ultimate form of storytelling. As I move through streets, what I see makes me think and get ideas for what I might next want to create, model, and move. I want nothing more from life than to wake up every day to do this work, collaborate with like-minded, obsessive devotees, and contribute all I can. I hope always to be surrounded by artists who are better, smarter, faster, and wiser, so I am forever learning. My greatest aim is to make movies that are thought-provoking, stimulate viewers' imaginations, and pose the question, "Imagine if . . . ."

To animate means to bring to life. When I make characters come to life, and every time I learn something new, I too come alive.[42]

---

42 The building blocks of Andreas's essay:
Five Best-Day Words: eager, determined, outgoing, calm, open
Story: dedicating himself to art and animation
Message: While bringing all I can imagine to life, I come alive.
Archetypes: Artist, Dreamer, Seeker

THINK OUTSIDE ANOTHER BOX

When Amanda wrote her Common App essay during a presidential election year, she couldn't keep her politics out of it. So she wrote her essay in the form of an open letter to the candidates and shared her personal story and dedication to inclusion and equality.

Amanda's Common App Essay

Dear Presidential Candidates,

I was outnumbered. My triplet brothers were born deeply connected. All the same age and with similar interests, they were the best of friends. Born two years later and given the title "the triplets' younger sister," I became the outcast fourth child.

Throughout my childhood, I wanted to join their games, but I felt overpowered. When we played basketball, they dangled the ball high above my head. When we played tag, I was always "it," because they ran faster. Every day, they teased me, saying "You run like a girl!" At the time, I didn't understand that they intended it as an insult. Finally, I had to make a choice: I could continue to allow them to exclude me, or I could "man up," as my brothers said, decide I was their equal, and make myself heard. I chose instead to "woman up."

For part of each day, I set aside my Barbies, insisted on playing sports with my brothers, and soon grew strong. At home, when the triplets teased me, I developed a thick skin. At the park, I became a fierce athlete and moved from the girls' basketball team to the boys' team. At school, when boys dismissed girls' ideas by saying "You're too bossy" and "You must be on your period," I felt moved to run for class president to defend and represent my gender.

For the past six years, I have attended Marlborough, an all-girls school where my classmates have become sisters rather than competitors. We've heard visiting speakers, including Condoleezza Rice and Madeleine Albright, discuss political activism for women's empowerment. I took a gender and sexuality class in which we explored gender roles in the past versus the present, read philosophy and theory texts, and studied the three waves of feminism. Throughout my six years, I learned that the true meaning of feminism is the belief in equal rights and opportunities for men and women, hardly an offensive ideal. Yet out in the world, I observed a sensitivity around the word and a frequent negative connotation associated with it. It reminded me of those playground insults that I had heard when I was a kid. I want to change the perception of the word "feminism." And I want you to help me.

You are running for a position that comes with power and influence. I ask you to be a leader I can look up to, one who believes that wearing a dress is unrelated to how well I might do my job, and one who supports my intention to raise kids and pursue a career and excel at both. Work to create a country in which it is socially acceptable for a man to stay at home while a woman strives toward her own professional goals. Commit yourself to commanding our troops, balancing the budget, getting Congress to agree, and making equal rights a top priority for everyone.

As I look ahead to college, I am eager to join a new community. There I will explore my interests in film, journalism, and international studies. I will seek out all kinds of people to discover our common ground. As a confident feminist with a powerful voice, I will stand up for the equality of men and women and work to create a vibrant, inclusive community for all students, even those who do not identify as male or female.

Yesterday, I rose to the challenges of growing up as the younger sister of triplet brothers. Today,

I appreciate all the ways that experience shaped and inspired me. Tomorrow, if the world should dangle opportunities for equality high above my head, I know I won't hesitate to jump. I encourage you to take that leap with me.

Sincerely,

A Young Feminist[43]

Do you have an idea to put your essay in an unexpected form? So long as it effectively tells your story and delivers your message—and doesn't turn into a gimmick—then go for it. Your reader will be happy to encounter something new.

---

43 The building blocks of Amanda's essay:
Five Best-Day Words: confident, outgoing, powerful, nice, ambitious
Story: letter to the candidates demanding action
Message: I dedicate myself to pursuing equality for all.
Archetypes: Leader, Adventurer, Hero

WHEN YOUR STORY IS BIGGER THAN A SINGLE MOMENT

While brainstorming an essay with a student named Erik, I was encouraging him to look for a single experience climaxing in a moment when he took a chance, overcame an obstacle, learned something significant, or changed in a meaningful way. But Erik had a problem. He knew he wanted to write about mountain biking, which had been his passion for eleven years. But over the course of all those years, he'd had dozens of textured and varied experiences that had taught him many different, important lessons. Every time he tried to narrow it down to a single experience, he felt he was losing the bigger picture.

In working with Erik, I was forced to admit that sometimes a long-term story is about more than a moment. Sometimes it is about the sum of many moments. The problem is that it's hard to generate much emotion when writing only about all the small parts that make up a larger whole. So Erik and I compromised. I suggested he use the first half of his essay to critically think and write about the many facets of his mountain biking experience. Then I asked him to use the second half to tell a single story that generates some suspense, illustrates him taking action, and ultimately moves both the writer and the reader. After much brainstorming, critical thinking, writing, winnowing, rewriting, trimming, and polishing, this is what he came up with.

Erik's Common App Essay

One of my earliest memories from childhood is being afraid to take the training wheels off my bike. I was six years old and terrified. After much convincing, I finally took my first two-wheeled ride. Soon after, my dad took me on a small mountain bike ride in the local hills, and I was hooked. Ever since, I've spent the last eleven years mountain biking and more recently training and competing.

This sport has helped me explore and appreciate the world around me. To me, that means learning the differences between suspension pivot points and dampening systems on the complex machine I spend so much time on. It's seeing the history and the beauty in century-old redwood trees that tower above the forest floor. It's meeting other mountain bikers from distant countries and cultures and, although not sharing the same language, sharing happy experiences together.

On a 90-degree summer day, struggling up a steep hillside under the hot sun is not the most pleasant activity. But for me, this is more enjoyable than simply arriving at the top of a mountain. As Ralph Waldo Emerson said, "Life is a journey, not a destination." Along the way, I've pushed my body to the limit for twelve hours each week, developed enormous self-discipline, and learned that working hard every day over time can produce concrete results, like winning my first downhill race last June and signing sponsorship contracts with major brands *GoPro* and *Spy Optics*.

Because I'm aware of the extreme risks associated with mountain biking, I've taken steps to make the sport I love a little safer. I've learned how to identify fractured clavicles and concussions. I've taken a first aid and CPR certification class twice to keep my knowledge up to date. I've stored mountain emergency numbers in my phone and always bring first aid supplies with me. While precautions like CPR certification might not do me much good if I were to get hurt, I've prepared this way in case something happens to a friend or stranger.

When I was just fifteen years old, my training proved useful. I was mountain biking at Big Bear, California, riding down an expert-level trail with lots of jumps. It was a quiet day, but ahead of me was one other rider, a man in his thirties. I was about fifty feet behind him when I saw him wipe out; I knew right away it would be bad.

Immediately, I blocked the path with my bike and instructed another cyclist to redirect riders around the accident. When I made my way down to the man, he was conscious and breathing but badly hurt. Making sure not to move him, I contacted the mountain emergency services and stayed with him until medical staff arrived. They concluded he'd suffered a spinal injury, loaded him in an ambulance, and took him down the mountain.

This experience shook me. It showed me the very real dangers of my sport. But it also revealed that I can contribute as much to an emergency situation as many adults. On that day, I felt proud to have made a difference. I know now that wherever I go, I can take decisive action as a committed and engaged member of my community and have a meaningful impact.

If I were asked what my single greatest talent is, I'd say mountain biking. Not purely because of my hard-earned technical skills on trails but also because of my ability to carry over lessons learned on the mountain to other parts of my life. Lessons about physics, nature, and different cultures shape the way I see the world, while my ongoing dedication to self-improvement and preparedness follows me into my academic studies and beyond. Now looking back, I'm so glad my dad convinced me to take off those training wheels all those years ago.[44]

---

44 The building blocks of Erik's essay:
Five Best-Day Words: driven, fearless, decisive, thoughtful, knowledge seeker
Story: mountain biking
Message: I seek challenges every day to grow and improve.
Archetypes: Seeker, Adventurer, Leader

Erik's essay is an exception to the rule that you should use your essay to tell a single story. It works because he shares so many compelling things that he's learned over time (the physics of his bike, his appreciation of nature, the pleasure he takes in meeting diverse cyclists, his profound work ethic, his successes, and his unusually mature dedication to safety and preparation). And then he shares a single story that illustrates how he takes thoughtful action in an emergency, which moves him and his reader. Finally, in his closing, he articulates his message: that he carries over all the lessons he's learned from years of mountain biking to achieve more in his academic studies and life. And he emotionally circles back to the image he opened with: the training wheels.

If you've had an experience that you've committed yourself to for many years, and you feel you can't fully share the larger experience by telling a single story, you might decide to broaden the canvas. If you do, be sure to illustrate yourself facing challenges, taking action, and changing. Remember to tell your story in a way that moves your reader. And, of course, by the time you reach the end of your essay, the many different moments must add up to a larger message: why this experience matters to you, how it changed you, and why it is vital to who you are and how you think and live.

THE EVOLUTION OF AN ESSAY

If you're looking for inspiration to keep working on and improving your essay until it succeeds on every level, look no further. When my student Cece arrived in my office, she had written her first draft independently. She knew it needed help, but she didn't know exactly how to proceed. That's when I came on board.

To illustrate our collaboration and how Cece's essay evolved, I am attaching the first draft that she wrote on her own, a new outline we created together to improve her structure, a transitional draft with my comments, and her final draft. My hope is that you'll see how I guided her to clarify her structure, tell a single story, declare her message, and heighten the feeling.

One note: when I first read Cece's original draft and realized she was writing her Common App essay about Instagram and her cell phone, I broke into a cold sweat. Students in Cece's generation are often attached to their devices and social media in ways that older readers are not, and I worried that a college admissions officer might dismiss Cece as superficial (the most important thing she has to write about is her cell phone??!!). But after I read the essay and understood the meaningful and substantive ways that Cece uses technology, I relaxed. Please take Cece's lesson to heart: if you must write about tech, show how you use it as a means to a much greater end.

Cece's Original Draft #1

A vibrant encapsulation of the busy yet iridescent chaos of Times Square in the wintertime. My guilty pleasure—coffee and chocolate ice cream bordered by two warm chocolate chip cookies. A photo of my dad and me—circa '99—in which I am struggling to free myself from the confinement of a pool floaty. My Instagram captures moments and memories of my life. I often find myself scrolling through the 122 weeks' worth of pictures to escape my current reality and to time-travel to some of my favorite experiences.

However, the pictures of my favorite lifestyle blogger, my 26-year-old co-worker, and my high school's Associated Student Body live on my feed too. Two toddlers in fluffy puffy jackets and duck-yellow rain boots cuddling under the Eiffel Tower, a video of a Filipino ballad, and a rambunctious Red Tide under the Friday night lights allow me to glimpse into others' experiences, experiences so different from yet similar to my own.

As I find new people to follow and pictures to examine, my mind expands to become less myopic and more cosmopolitan, rich with the vast array of ways to live life. Through a few colorful and anecdotal images, I know what it is like to live in New York City and raise a family, to have talented vocal chords, and to be the painted-red face of a school—all things I have imagined and dreamed of doing. I guess that is why I find myself perfectly content in the world of a 5×2-inch piece of metal.

A man playing a horn, Peruvian women dressed in colonial garb, and the picturesque landscape of Machu Picchu take residence on the homepage for the Andean Masters Institute in Cusco, Peru. The paqos Rodolfo and Adolfo too benefit from technological portals in which they can share and celebrate their personal and unique situations. For them, two spiritual leaders dedicated to preserving and teaching the traditions of their Andean ancestors, I created a website to promote and inform about the institute in progress. They are grounded by their dedication to the earth, yet they also find solace through the spreading of their messages, though it may be through a web of interconnected computer networks. I have enjoyed the intimate view I have gotten of their very different, yet modest, natural, and kind way of life. They can now share their lifestyle through an all-encapsulating website, as I do mine via a few square-shaped photos.

And through technological portals like Instagram, I am still left intrigued. If I search hard enough, there is a photograph or account for all of my little interests and quirks—for my obsession with big furry dogs, my foodie-ness, my favorite volleyball player, and for the funniest character on The Office. I am reminded of these things as I reprimand myself for spending too much time on my phone, and then I no longer regret my procrastination.

As society becomes more afraid of our advancing technological world, I will be sitting front row with a bag of buttered popcorn and a pack of Junior Mints. I am excited for the developments to be made and can only hope I am behind them in the future, because I am grateful for the moments and memories I can share and vicariously receive.

After reading and discussing the draft with Cece, we agreed that the essay spent too many words on her phone and not enough on how she engages in life. The draft jumped around and lacked a single, chronological story with a clear beginning, middle, and ending that illustrates how Cece operates in the world. Finally, it needed a more clearly declared message and more open emotion.

Before Cece wrote her next draft, we created a new structure/outline for her to work from.

Outline for Cece's Next Draft

OPENING (200 words)
Paragraph 1:
Ex. 1: The busy yet iridescent chaos of Times Square in the wintertime.

Ex. 2: Coffee chip ice cream bordered by two warm chocolate chip cookies.

Ex. 3: My dad and me, circa '99, as I struggle to free myself from the confinement of a pool floaty.

Summary: My cell phone captures moments and memories of my life.

Paragraph 2:
However, cell phone doesn't just provide view of my experiences.
Also offers glimpse of others' experiences out in world.
Ex. 1
Ex. 2
Ex. 3
As I find new people to follow and pictures to examine, my phone expands my mind to become less myopic and more cosmopolitan, rich with the vast array of ways to live life.

Paragraph 3:
My cell phone is a window onto the world.
Yet even beyond accessing my own and others'

content, phone offers one more profound gift: opportunity to change that world by creating content. This is use that most excites me.

BODY: PERU STORY (300 words)

Paragraph 1:

Years ago, aunt went to Peru, met paqos Rodolfo and Adolfo, embraced their spiritual path.

Came home, wrote two books on them.

As I discussed with my aunt, I grew interested.

Learned they live a kind, modest, natural life grounded by their devotion to the earth and the conservation of the traditions of their Andean ancestors.

When the paqos were visiting the US, lucky to travel with aunt to meet them in Colorado.

Discovered they were creating the Andean Masters Institute in Cuzco that would be center for research and teaching, but had no way to share information with outside world.

Paragraph 2:

Around same time, wrote a paper in school on how I believe advancing technology can be used to benefit people trying to conserve traditional ways of life.

Realized I had opportunity to test my theory and help these people in meaningful way.

This fall, designed a website for the paqos to use as a platform to promote and inform about the institute.

Describe website photos.

Describe website videos.

Describe website links.

Created a technological portal that celebrated their unique experiences and beliefs.

Used my new world skills to honor and protect their old-world history and customs.

CLOSING (150 WORDS)

Paragraph 1:

I believe technology is a beautiful, powerful thing.

Allows me to share and receive content with loved ones and strangers.

Enables me to make connections that would otherwise be out of reach.

Gives me means to make a difference.

Know now that technology doesn't threaten old ways of life.

Rather offers means to keep them alive.

Paragraph 2:

Though some in society are growing more and more afraid of our modern world, I am becoming more and more grateful for the unprecedented access it provides.

As technology advances, I am excited for the developments to come.

Can't wait for future when won't just appreciate innovations but will participate in their creation.

Jumping ahead a few drafts, Cece had made much progress but still wasn't all the way there. Take a look at draft #4 (with my notes in *italics*).

Cece's Draft #4

OPENING

A vibrant encapsulation of the iridescent chaos of Times Square. My guilty pleasure—coffee and chocolate chip ice cream bordered by two chocolate chip cookies. A photo of my dad and me—circa '99—in which I struggle to free myself from the confinement of a pool floaty. My Instagram captures moments and memories of my life. I often find myself scrolling through the 122 weeks' worth of pictures to time-travel to some of my favorite experiences. *(Cece, please trim the three glimpses and eliminate references to them being encapsulations or photos. I think they will be more dynamic if you just let them be quick, cinematic "shots." Then end the paragraph with one sentence explaining that your Instagram helps you look inward.)*

The pictures of my favorite lifestyle blogger, my singing 26-year-old co-worker, and my high school's Associated Student Body live on my feed too. Through a few colorful and anecdotal images, I glimpse into others' experiences, experiences so different from yet similar to my own. My mind expands to become less myopic and more cosmopolitan. *(For your second paragraph, offer three quick, vibrant cinematic shots that move you out into the world: start on a local stage [your high school community], then move to a national stage [perhaps your favorite lifestyle blogger?], and for the third one choose something international [something that authentically interests you]. This will reveal that you are curious about and paying attention to the larger world and thinking about issues larger than your single life [something colleges get excited about]. Then summarize that you also use your phone to look outward.)*

My cell phone is my virtual window onto the world, and I am a believer of technology. Beyond offering me an opportunity to reflect inwardly on my own content and to look outwardly on others', it most importantly offers me an opportunity to create content for the world. *(Perhaps trim "and I am a believer of technology" because it interrupts your train of thought. Maybe you can save and use that idea somewhere in your conclusion? Also, please add a sentence about how you feel about the opportunity to create content for the world. Is this exciting for you? This is where you want to start to share/ express/reveal your passion.)*

PERU STORY

My zany aunt became infatuated with the spiritual denomination of an Incan community she had crossed paths with on a spontaneous journey to Peru. She would email me the messages she had received from the paqos Rodolfo and Adolfo, the spiritual leaders of the community, so I was eventually recruited as her Spanish translator ("Cece, how do I use Google Translate?" she once asked). After communicating with the paqos for several months, I began to communicate with them independently and learned that they were building an institute in Cuzco, Peru, to be a center for research and the teaching of their beliefs. However, they lacked the means to successfully inform the outside world. *(Start paragraph with a quick transition, maybe telling when this happened? Maybe don't refer to your aunt as zany because her zaniness might reflect poorly on the Peruvians? You mentioned to me that your aunt wrote a couple books about them. Maybe include that to give it more substance?)*

I met the paqos in Denver on their first-ever journey together to America and spent a week inhaling the messages they breathe—the importance of society's devotion to the earth and of conserving traditions like those of their Andean ancestors. After getting an intimate view of their lifestyles and receiving such a warm and kind embrace from their community, I felt inclined to spread the awareness of the institute they were creating. My technologically-crazed mind embarked on a project: a website to promote and inform about the Andean Masters Institute and the belief system that will be taught there. Pictures of the beautiful garb *(more details to come)* live on the website, where they now have the opportunity to share and celebrate their own unique way of life. A way of life so ancient and fragile that can now be preserved by a progressive system of interconnected computer networks. *(Try moving the last two sentences of this paragraph into the beginning of the next paragraph and unfurl the whole story of building the website. Include colorful, specific details of the website content.)*

Never had I thought that my tech-savvy-ness would lead me to make a connection with a community 4,468 miles away. I knew I made a difference when Rodolfo emailed me, on his newly established email account I might add, thanking me on behalf of the community for my kind heart. I had never realized that my fascination with technology could actually manifest into a project that would change people's lives. And the true beauty of the experience was that their histories and customs are respectfully preserved by a modern advancement that will only keep those things alive. *(Touch back on how this experience moved you. Every aspect of this story should be filtered through how the experience had an impact on you. And tell the story chronologically as much as possible.)*

CLOSING

Technology is beautiful to me because it has allowed me to make connections I would have never made otherwise, to make a meaningful difference, and to become much more culturally and worldly aware—whether it be of the inhabitants of Peru or of the people on my Instagram feed. Though society is becoming more and more afraid of our modern world, I am becoming more grateful for the new opportunities, information, and cultural enlightenment we now have access to. I am excited for the developments to be made and cannot wait to be behind them in the future. *(Be careful to eliminate any repetition. Use your first sentence to declare a real and specific message [I believe that technology is a beautiful thing!]. Try not to repeat what you have already said and illustrated. Use these words to go somewhere new. I like that you circled back to the Instagram reference from your opening. I think your essay needs to be more emotional at the end, connect more expressively to your excitement and feelings about these possibilities. Ultimately, you should aim to expand your closing. Once we get the content right for every section, then we will trim it down to proper length.)*

Cece made all these changes. Together we then polished her writing, eliminated repetition, proofread, and trimmed the essay to 649 words. Here is her final draft. I hope it motivates you to work through many drafts to the best version of an authentic, meaningful, moving Common App essay of your own.

Cece's Final Draft #8

The iridescent chaos of Times Square in wintertime. My guilty pleasure—coffee ice cream bordered by two chocolate chip cookies. My dad and me—circa '99—in which I struggle to free myself from the confinement of a pool floaty. My Instagram captures moments and memories of my life and allows me to time-travel to some of my favorite experiences.[45]

My high school's rambunctious Red Tide under the Friday night lights. "Taza's New York City Guide" published by my favorite lifestyle blogger. A young Afghan woman embracing a National Geographic journalist, captioned "#tooyoungtowed." Through colorful images and anecdotal videos that too live on my feed, I get a glimpse into others' experiences. My mind happily expands to become less myopic, more cosmopolitan, and engaged with the vast array of circumstances and challenges faced around the world.

My cell phone is my virtual window onto the world. It offers me an opportunity to reflect inward on my own content and to look outward on others'. But most excitingly, it offers me an opportunity to create impactful content. I come alive on

---

45 Can we take a moment to admire the final draft of Cece's opening? She took a chance and fearlessly launched her essay with quick and colorful jump cuts of images that flash across her screens. By starting with bold images and vivid language in sentence fragments, she confidently let the reader know upfront that this essay would be different, as is she. She made her writing style match her personal style and theme.

the promise that, with a few simple clicks of a keyboard, I can change the world.

A few years ago, my aunt grew interested in the spiritual denomination of an Incan community dedicated to the teaching and preservation of the traditions of their Andean ancestors. She had crossed paths with the group's leaders, Rodolfo and Adolfo, on a spontaneous journey to Peru, and she ultimately wrote two books about them. When she received messages from them, she would email them to me to translate from Spanish. After helping her communicate with them for several months, I began to communicate with them independently and learned that they were building an institute in Cuzco, Peru, to be a center for research and the teaching of their beliefs. However, they lacked the means to successfully inform the outside world.

When Rodolfo and Adolfo made their first-ever journey together to America, I met them in Denver and spent a week inhaling the profound messages they breathe: the importance of society's devotion to the earth and of conserving traditions like those of their ancestors. After getting an intimate view of their lifestyle and values and receiving such a warm and kind embrace from their community, I wanted to help them spread awareness of the institute they were creating. That is when my technologically crazed mind decided to create a website to promote and inform about the Andean Masters Institute and the belief system that will be taught there.

I dove into the project and began to fill the website with images of Peruvian women in vibrant traditional garb, biographies of the institute's masters, and descriptions of their mission, values, and vision for the school. Before embarking on this effort, I had never imagined that my tech-savviness would lead me to make a connection with a community 4,468 miles away. But as I helped these people share and celebrate their ancient and fragile way of life via a progressive system of interconnected computer networks, I was thrilled to discover that I could keep alive the history and customs that mean so much to them through the modern advancements that mean so much to me. When Rodolfo emailed me, thanking me on behalf of the community for my kind heart, I knew I had taken part in something truly meaningful.

I believe that technology is a beautiful thing. It has allowed me to reach out and connect to others, whether they be the indigenous people of Peru or the colorful crowd on my Instagram feed. Though many in society grow more afraid of our modern world, I grow more grateful for the new opportunities, information, and cultural enlightenment we now have access to. I am excited for the revolutionary developments that will be made and cannot wait to be at the forefront of them in the future.[46]

---

46 The building blocks of Cece's essay:
Five Best-Day Words: ambitious, generous, warm, inclusive, driven
Story: building a website for the Peruvians
Message: I find meaning and purpose in using technology to connect people.
Archetypes: Seeker, Adventurer

WHERE'D THEY LAND?

I'd like to thank all the generous students who granted me permission to include their essays, opening sentences, messages, and experiences with you in this book so you could learn from their work. If you're curious where the essay writers landed for college, satisfy your curiosity here. And know that each one ended up at a school that deeply valued them for who they are and what they offered. I wish you all the same success.

STUDENT	ESSAY	COLLEGE
Abby	corn maze	Chapman College
Jackson	building steps	University of California, Berkeley
Ella	Black Lives Matter	Amherst College
Molly	quitting swim team	Occidental College
Josh	doing good	pending at time of publication
Cole	pizza job	Sonoma State University

Nathan	Parisian grandfather	Reed College
Annie	video class	University of Michigan
Samuel	fantasy football	University of Oregon
Winnie	Sea Scouts	University of California, Berkeley
Grant	composer	Harvard University
Tess	moving with mom	Kenyon College
Chloe	cheer	University of California, Santa Cruz
Female Hero	anorexia	University of Puget Sound
Male Hero	political debate	University of Virginia
Female Seeker	forensic pathologist	Northeastern University
Male Seeker	building a catamaran	Pitzer College
Female Adventurer	Boeing internship	University of Southern California

Male Adventurer	day in Australia	University of California, Berkeley
Female Rebel	high school anomaly	University of Washington
Male Rebel	business	University of Southern California
Female Dreamer	Teen Line	Wellesley College
Male Dreamer	gardener	St. Olaf College
Female Caregiver	brother in rehab	Boston University
Male Caregiver	soccer coach	Indiana University, Bloomington
Female Artist	photographer	McGill University
Male Artist	filmmaker	Sarah Lawrence College
Female Leader	theater	Brandeis University
Male Leader	lacrosse captain	Washington and Lee University

Zianna	Hollywood Bowl	New York University
Fiona	Starbucks	University of Michigan
Brian	dyslexia	University of Southern California
Siena	Berlin internship	Savannah College of Art and Design
Andreas	animation	New York University
Amanda	letter to candidates	University of Southern California
Erik	mountain biking	University of California, Santa Cruz
Cece	website for Peruvians	Massachusetts Institute of Technology

BIG THANKS

There are many people who helped make this book possible and deserve my heartfelt thanks:

• my brother, Steve Ferber, who made a phone call on a late December night to ask for my help with his niece's essay. Who knew where that would lead?!

• my students over the years, who met me with open hearts and minds and allowed me the privilege of helping them help themselves;

• my early readers--Steven Frank, Sophie Frank, Michael Frank, Jo Anne Schlesinger, Ali Peters, and Scout Turkel— whose time, energy, and thoughtful feedback made each draft stronger;

• my agent, Kevin O'Connor, of O'Connor Literary Agency, who read my manuscript, believed in it, and didn't give up until we found it a proper home;

• my editor, Eliza Berkowitz, of Sterling Children's Books/ Sterling Publishing Co., whose keen insights, respect, and enthusiasm shined through in every interaction;

• the book's art director and cover designer, Irene Vandervoort; project editor, Hannah Reich; and production manager, Terence Campo, who turned a file on my laptop into a beautiful book I can hold;

• and, finally, to my husband and kids, who muster patience when my students draw my attention away from them and offer me love, encouragement, and humor just when I need it most.

INDEX

A

Abby's essay, 36–41
Academics, listing, 134
Actions, taking
  essay analysis showing, 50
  words that matter and, 17, 132
Adaptability
  colleges looking for students with, 20
  essay analyses showing, 50, 93
  words that matter and, 16, 131
Adventurer archetype
  characteristics, 32
  essays by writer identifying with, 36–41, 75–78, 83–85, 86–89, 211–214, 218–221, 222–226, 239–242
  sample essay (male), 168–171
  sample essays (female), 36–41, 165–168
  writing essay as, 34–35
Amanda's essay, 218–221
Andrea's essay, 215–217
Annie's essay, 86–89
Archetype(s). See also specific archetypes
  about: overview of, 30–33
  assessing which sound like you, 31–32
  as building block of essay, 30–35
  defined, 30
  figuring out who you are and revealing in story, 34–35, 135
  sample essays by type of. See specific archetypes
  types of, thumbnail sketches, 32
  as your brand, 33
Artist archetype
  characteristics, 32
  essays by writer identifying with, 70–74, 75–78, 83–85, 86–89, 116–120, 121–124, 206–210, 215–217
  sample essay (female), 192–195
  sample essay (male), 195–198

Art school, essay example for, 215–217
Attention, grabbing reader's, 50, 98, 101, 108, 140–141
Authenticity
  essay analyses showing, 39, 50, 108
  sample essay (male), 195–198
  of story, 23
  of voice, 39, 140
  words that matter and, 16, 131

B

Beginning, middle, ending. See also Structure of essay (opening, body, closing)
  essay analyses showing, 39, 44, 50, 62, 97, 98, 99
  problem, struggle/growth, resolution and, 96, 138, 140
  sample structures illustrating, 97–99
  step-by-step guide and, 138, 140
  words that matter and, 17, 132
Best-day words. See Five best-day words, sample essays using; Five words
Body of essay. See Structure of essay (opening, body, closing)
Brian's essay, 79, 80–82
Bridge-building, 16, 40, 50, 131
Building blocks of essays, 22–35. See also specific building blocks
  about: bouncing between, 94
  #1: Five words, 22–23
  #2: Story, 23–25
  #3: Message, 25–30
  #4 Archetype, 30–35

C

Caregiver archetype
  characteristics, 32
  essays by writer identifying with, 46–51, 58–63, 70–74
  sample essay (female), 186–188
  sample essay (male), 189–191

Challenges. *See* Conflict and challenges
Change, willingness to embrace
  Erik's Essay, 222–226
  essay analysis showing, 51
  essays by archetype illustrating. *See specific archetypes*
  story illustrating, 25
  words that matter and, 16, 131
Character
  colleges looking for students with, 19
  defined, 19
  essay analysis showing, 50
  story revealing, 23–24
  words that matter and, 16, 131
Chloe's essay, 126–130
Circling back, 45, 78, 100, 141
Clarity of writing, 39, 141
Closing of essay. *See* Structure of essay (opening, body, closing)
Cole's Essay, 70–74, 99. *See also* Fiona's essay
College(s)
  articulating why you want to go, 134
  what they look for in applicants, 19–20
  where students writing essays in this book landed, 243–246
Common App essays
  about: overview of writing, 13–15
  author's story, 9–11
  optimizing your opportunity, 130–133
  prompts, 19, 134
  revising. *See* Drafts and revisions
  rounding out picture of yourself, 130–131
  step by step. *See* Step-by-step guide; *specific steps*
  supplemental essays and, 49n7, 144–145
  topics for, 130
  what they should do for you, 21
  words that matter, 16–17, 131–132
Confidence
  essay analyses showing, 39, 44–45
  words that matter and, 16, 132

Conflict and challenges
  Erik's Essay, 222–226
  essay analyses showing, 39, 44
  essays by archetype illustrating. *See specific archetypes*
  responding to. *See* Adaptability; Resilience
  story including, 25, 140. *See also* Beginning, middle, ending
  words that matter and, 16, 131
Conversational voice, 39, 140
Courage, 120–124
Creativity
  Andrea's essay, 215–217
  Annie's essay, 85–89
  discovering yours, 137
  step-by-step guide and, 137
  topics based on, 86–89
  words that matter and, 17, 132

D

Dedication, 20, 93
Details
  courage, 120–124
  first sentence, 108–112, 140–141
  framing device, 125–130, 138–139
  quotes, 112–113, 141
  voice, 107–108
Dialogue, 45, 140
Diversity, embracing, 16, 20, 40, 50, 131
Drafts and revisions
  first, 139
  getting feedback, 142–143
  rewriting, 139–141, 143
Drafts and revisions, Cece's example, 227–241
  about: overview of, 227
  draft #1, 228–230
  draft #4, 234–239
  draft #8 (final), 239–242
  outline for draft #2, 231–234
Dreamer archetype
  characteristics, 32
  essays by writer identifying with, 58–63, 126–130, 206–210, 215–217
  sample essay (female), 179–181
  sample essay (male), 182–185
Dyslexia, overcoming, 79, 80–82

250

E

Ella's essay, 46–51
Emotion/feeling, 113–120
  accessing and expressing
    effectively, 114–116
  Grant's essay expressing, 116–120
  importance of writing with,
    113–114
  small moments adding up to bigger
    realization, 114–115
  story revealing, 23, 140
  words that matter and, 16, 131
Erik's Essay, 222–226
Experience. *See* Message; Story
Extracurriculars, listing, 134

F

Feedback, getting, 142–143
Feeling. *See* Emotion/feeling
Fiona's essay, 211–214
First sentence, 108–112
  checking, 140–141
  examples, 108–111
  importance of, 108, 111–112
Five best-day words, sample essays
    using
  adventurous, curious, energetic,
    musical, passionate, 75–78
  ambitious, generous, warm,
    inclusive, driven, 239–242
  ambitious, open minded,
    independent, disciplined,
    creative, 41–46
  ambitious, thoughtful, funny,
    sensitive, intuitive, 103–106
  artistic, dedicated, open, sensitive,
    curious, 121–124
  charismatic, hardworking,
    understanding, funny,
    contemplative, 46–51
  confident, outgoing, powerful,
    nice, ambitious, 218–221
  creative, passionate, fearless, fun,
    capable, 83–85
  creative, present, engaged, curious,
    joyful, 206–210
  creative, strong, sensitive, joyful,
    connected, 85–89
  driven, fearless, decisive,
    thoughtful, knowledge seeker,
    222–226
  eager, determined, outgoing, calm,
    open, 215–217
  fun, ambitious, social, athletic,
    motivated, 90–93
  happy, funny, passionate, kind,
    caring, 58–63
  independent, ambitious,
    open-minded, friendly,
    compassionate, 211–214
  kind, gentle, lively, brave, joyful,
    126–130
  kind, helpful, hardworking,
    creative, athletic, 80–82
  outgoing, generous, thoughtful,
    intelligent, hardworking,
    116–120
  outgoing, upbeat, diligent, curious,
    kind, 36–41
  thoughtful, ambitious, committed,
    optimistic, generous, 65–69
  warm, funny, smart, outgoing,
    caring, 70–74
Five words
  as building block of essay, 22–23
  describing you on best day, 22, 134.
    See also Five best-day words,
    sample essays using
  describing you on worst day, 23, 135
  step-by-step guide and, 134–135
Focus
  essay analysis showing, 93
  showing quality of, 93
Focusing on yourself, 51, 57n9,
    191n38
Framing device, 125–130, 138–139

G

Generosity
  colleges looking for dedication and,
    20
  essay analysis showing, 50
  words that matter and, 16, 131
Grabbing reader's attention, 50, 98,
    101, 108, 140–141
Grant's essay, 116–120, 142n33
Growth
  essay analysis showing, 51
  essays by archetype illustrating. *See*
    specific archetypes
  story including, 25
  words that matter and, 16, 132

H

Hero archetype
  characteristics, 32
  essays by writer identifying with,
    41–46, 80–82, 83–85, 90–93,
    103–106, 121–124, 126–130,
    218–221
  sample essay (female), 151–153
  sample essay (male), 154–157
Honesty
  essay analysis showing, 39–40
  words that matter and, 17, 132
Humor
  essay analyses showing, 40, 46
  words that matter and, 17, 132

I

Imagery, 39, 140
Impact
  big, 57–63, 135–136
  discovering yours, 135–136
  essay analysis showing, 50
  Molly's essay, 58–63
  step-by-step guide and, 135–136
  words that matter and, 16, 132
Intellectual vitality
  colleges looking for students with,
    20
  defined, 20
  discovering yours, 136
  essay analysis showing, 46
  Nathan's essay illustrating, 75–78
  step-by-step guide and, 136
  story illustrating, 23
  topics based on, 74–78
  words that matter and, 16, 131

J

Jackson's essay, 41–46, 97
Josh's essay, 65–69

L

Leader archetype
  characteristics, 32
  essays by writer identifying with,
    36–41, 41–46, 46–51, 65–69,
    70–74, 116–119, 211–214,
    218–221, 222–226
  sample essay (female), 199–202
  sample essay (male), 202–205

Leadership qualities
  story illustrating, 24–25
  words that matter and, 16, 131
Learning differences, 79–85, 136
Limit, word, precaution on, 143

M

Message
  as building block of essay, 25–30
  discovering, 26–28, 137–138
  essay analysis showing, 41
  importance and reason for, 25–27
  Rosie's example, 26–30
  step-by-step guide and, 137–138,
    141
  words that matter and, 16, 131
Message, essay samples by
  bringing all I can imagine to life, I
    come to life, 215–217
  dedicating self to pursuing equality
    for all, 218–221
  embracing challenge/risk and
    friendship, 103–106
  embracing uncertainty, 85–89
  everywhere I go, I try to do good,
    65–69
  finding meaning/purpose in
    technology to connect people,
    239–242
  living openly/outwardly to live life
    to fullest, 126–130
  living with intention/authenticity,
    willing to leave past behind,
    58–63
  music as greatest force in life,
    116–120
  owning choices/responsibilities for
    meaningful life, 121–124
  passionately seeking new ideas/
    ways of thinking daily, 75–78
  passion drives success, 90–93
  positive attitude will help take
    world by storm, 70–74
  pursuing beauty/great stories/
    truth with joy/nerve/curiosity,
    83–85
  pursuing excellence giving my life
    meaning, 41–46
  respect and curiosity when meeting
    everyone, 211–214

252

seeking challenges every day to grow and improve, 222–226
striving to learn always, 206–210
taking nothing for granted, working daily for growth, 80–82
wanting to reach out, connect with all types of people, 36–41
working to help my community survive, thrive, grow, 46–51
Molly's essay, 58–63, 98

N

Nathan's essay, 75–78

O

Obstacles. *See* Conflict and challenges
Obstacles/challenges, 25
Opening of essay. *See* Structure of essay (opening, body, closing)
Outlining essay, 95–106. *See also* Structure of essay (opening, body, closing)
about: overview of, 95–97
general guidelines, 138
step-by-step guide and, 138
tense and, 101–106
Outside-the-box thinking, 90–93, 137, 218–221

P

Passion
colleges looking for students with, 20
defined, 20
essay analyses showing, 44, 50, 89
words that matter and, 16, 131
Point of view
factors influencing, 64–65
step-by-step guide and, 136
unique, 36, 63–69, 89
Positive, accentuating, 69–74, 136
Prompts, Common App essay, 19, 134
Prompts, story, 52–53, 135
Proofing essay. *See* Drafts and revisions
Purpose
colleges looking for students with, 20
defined, 20
essay analysis showing, 50

story revealing, 23–24
words that matter and, 16, 131

Q

Questions, to find your topic/story, 53–57
Quotes, using, 112–113, 141
Rebel archetype
characteristics, 32
essay by writer identifying with, 90–93
sample essay (female), 172–175
sample essay (male), 175–178
Relationship with world, 40
Resilience
colleges looking for students with, 20
essay analyses showing, 50, 93
story illustrating, 25
words that matter and, 16, 131
Resolution, 96, 138, 140
Revising essay. *See* Drafts and revisions
Rosie's story, 26–30
Rounding out picture of yourself, 130–131

S

Sample essays and analysis (by writer)
Abby's essay, 36–41
Amanda's essay, 218–221
Andrea's essay, 215–217
Annie's essay, 86–89
Brian's essay, 79, 80–82
Cece's essay, 239–242. *See also* Drafts and revisions, Cece's example
Chloe's essay, 126–130
Cole's Essay, 70–74, 99. *See also* Fiona's essay
Ella's essay, 46–51
Erik's Essay, 222–226
Fiona's essay, 211–214
Grant's essay, 116–120, 142n33
Jackson's essay, 41–46, 97
Josh's essay, 65–69
Molly's essay, 58–62, 98
Nathan's essay, 75–78
Samuel's essay, 90–93
Siena's essay, 79, 83–85

Sample essays (*continued*)
  Tess's essay, 121–124
  Winnie's essay, 103–106
  Zianna's essay, 206–210
Samuel's essay, 90–93
Seeker archetype
  characteristics, 32
  essays by writer identifying with,
    36–41, 41–46, 65–69, 75–78,
    80–82, 86–89, 90–93, 103–106,
    116–120, 121–124, 126–130,
    206–210, 211–214, 215–217,
    222–226, 239–242
  sample essay (female), 158–161
  sample essay (male), 161–164
Sentences
  first, 108–112, 140–141
  varying language, length and style,
    141
  varying length, essay showing, 45
Service, pattern of, 132
Siena's essay, 79, 83–85
Sophie, 13, 113–114, 147–148,
    149n35
Specifics, essay analysis showing, 51
Step-by-step guide, 134–143. *See also*
    specific topics for elaboration on
    steps
  academics (listing), 134
  accentuating the positive, 136
  archetype identification, 135
  Common App essay prompts and,
    134
  creativity, 137
  dialogue, 140
  extracurriculars (listing), 134
  final checks and submitting essay,
    143
  first draft, rewrite, and polish,
    139–142
  five best-day words, 134
  five worst-day words, 135
  framing device, 138–139
  getting feedback, 142
  impact discovery, 135–136
  intellectual vitality, 136
  learning differences, 136
  message, 137–138, 141
  opening, body, closing, 138
  outline and structure, 138
  rationale for attending college, 134

story prompts, 135
  thinking outside the box, 137
  unique point of view, 136
  word budget by section, 138
  word limit precaution, 143
Story
  appeal of, 23
  as building block of essay, 23–25
  chronological progression. *See*
    Beginning, middle, ending
  Common App essay prompts and,
    19, 134
  figuring out who you are and
    revealing in, 34–35
  prompts, 52–53, 135
  qualities and characteristics to
    include, 23–25
  reason for writing, 23
  rounding out picture of yourself,
    130–131
  topics to use/avoid, 130
Story, essay samples by
  actively exploring world, 206–210
  building stone steps, 41–46
  building website for Peruvians,
    239–242
  camp counselor (empowering
    students of color), 46–51
  composer attending composition
    program, 116–120
  corn maze (bringing friends
    together), 36–41
  dedicating self to art/animation,
    215–217
  doing good in all parts of life, 65–69
  fantasy football league, 90–93
  grandfather sparking intellectual
    curiosity, 75–78
  internship in Berlin, 83–85
  letter to candidates demanding
    action, 218–221
  mountain biking, 222–226
  overcoming dyslexia, 79, 80–82
  overcoming family struggles,
    investing in self, 121–124
  pizza joint job, 70–74. *See also*
    Starbucks job
  quitting gymnastics and starting
    cheer, 126–130
  quitting swim team, 58–63
  Sea Scouts Fleet Drill, 103–106

Starbucks job, 211–214
video class/project, 85–89
Straightforwardness of writing, 141
Strengths, essay highlighting. *See*
    Abby's essay
Structure of essay (opening, body,
    closing). *See also* Beginning,
    middle, ending
  about: overview of, 95–97
  approaches and general guidelines,
    96–97, 138
  beginning, middle, ending, 138, 140
  circling back, 45, 78, 100, 141
  Cole's example, 99
  definition and functions of
    components, 95–97
  Grant's essay, 116–120, 142n33
  Jackson's example, 97
  Molly's example, 98
  revising. *See* Drafts and revisions
  samples, 97–99
  step-by-step guide and, 138
  tense and, 101–106
  word budgets, allocation by
    section, 99–101, 138
Struggles
  essay analyses showing, 40, 50
  story including, 25, 140
  words that matter and, 16, 131
Submitting essay, 143
Supplemental essays, 49n7, 144–145
Suspense
  essay analyses showing, 39, 44
  heightening, 140
  words that matter and, 16, 131

T
Tense of essay, 101–106
  past tense, 102–103
  power of, 101–102
  present tense, 101–102
  varying between present and past,
    103–106, 140
  Winnie's essay, 103–106
Tess's essay, 121–124
Topic, finding
  accentuating the positive and, 69–74
  big impacts and, 57–63
  Common App essay prompts and,
    19, 134
  creativity and, 86–89

intellectual vitality and, 74–78
learning differences and, 79–85, 136
perspective on, 94
questions to ask for, 53–57
story prompts and, 52–53, 135
thinking outside the box, 90–93, 137
unique point of view and, 63–69
Topics, of sample essays. *See* Story,
    essay samples by

U
Understanding, new. *See also* Change,
    willingness to embrace
  essays by archetype illustrating. *See*
    specific archetypes
  story including, 25
  words that matter and, 16, 132
Understatement, 45–46
Unique point of view, 63–69
  art-related schools and, 89
  discovering yours, 136
  Josh's essay, 65–69
  perfect pitch example, 64–65
  step-by-step guide and, 136
  Zianna's essay, 206–210
Unique quality
  story revealing, 25
  words that matter and, 17, 132

V
Voice, 107–108
  authentic, 39, 140
  confident. *See* Confidence
  conversational, 39, 140
  explained, 107
  unique, 44–45, 108
  as word that matters, 17, 132
  yours, writing your essay using, 108

W
Winnie's essay, 103–106
Word budgets, 99–101, 138
Word limit precaution, 143
Words that matter, 16–17, 131–132
Work ethic
  essay analyses showing, 46, 89
  words that matter and, 16, 131
Worst-day words, 23, 135

Z
Zianna's essay, 206–210